GW00771517

The Intelligent Citizen's Guide to Risks in Financial Institutions

Mark J Dougherty
Yan Fishman

Along with air, earth, water, and fire, money is the fifth
natural force a human being has to reckon with most often.
Joseph Brodsky, Russian-American Poet.

Money is the mysterious fifth element:
the quintessential ingredient of our reality.

Published by

JustWrite Technical Documentation,
Cheltenham GL51 9QS England

First published in 2014

ISBN 978-0-9928418-0-5

Acknowledgments

The authors would like to give their special thanks to
Tatiana Fishman for her art work on the book cover as well as
Sarah E. Dougherty and Michael J. Dougherty for their editing of
the early versions of the manuscript.

The authors

Mark Dougherty

Mark Dougherty is a professional accountant, a member of the Certified Management Accountants of Canada and an International Associate of the American Institute of Certified Public Accountants.

As a senior corporate governance and risk management professional, Mark has expertise in leading all aspects of credit, insurance market and operational risks initiatives for multi-billion dollar financial institutions. These initiatives, in Canada, United States, Europe and Asia, have included risk management, governance and regulatory best practices such as methodologies, models, systems policies and procedures.

Yan Fishman

Yan Fishman ISP, ITCP/IP3P is a senior business analysis and software development professional specializing in the computer assisted solutions for the financial institutions. He has had a leading position in the development of a mortgage control system for a major savings and loan corporation.

Yan has led the development of the systems for the Brady bonds credit and accounting for a major Canadian bank. He has designed, developed and implemented computer based credit risk models for the variety of the major bank business lines.

Overview

This book provides the intelligent average citizen (that is, a person having good judgment and sound thinking) with a thorough understanding of risks in financial institutions.

You will learn about:

- Risks, risk management and the risk management framework.
- Structured approaches on how to identify, analyse, monitor, manage and report key risks.
- Benefits of good risk management.
- How financial institutions can mitigate or control risks.
- How capital provides support to moderate risks.
- How to use all necessary information to make an informed decision on risks and capital.

And you will be given practical guidance on the subject of risk.

This book discusses the concepts of risk and related matters through the eyes of a man by the name of Luca Pacioli. Pacioli (1445-1517) was an Italian mathematician and Franciscan friar who outlined and described a system of double entry book-keeping which is still in use today.

This book assumes that Pacioli has been in a deep sleep since for around 500 years and has now been awakened in the early 21st century. What would Pacioli think of risk today?

Key concepts of risk, risk management and financial institutions

The term "risk" comes from the Italian word "*risicare*" meaning "dare". This is fitting in the context of the modern financial marketplace since risk management requires the daring to act and decide what sorts of financial activities should be carried out.

Risk can be defined in terms of the totality of expected and unexpected losses. Expected losses are changes in values that can be derived from information currently anticipated, while unexpected losses are deviations from the expected losses or gains.

The successful delivery of an organization's objectives is impacted by the inherent uncertainty of the business environment or, said another way, risk. Thus, risk can be conceived as both hazard and opportunity. "Risk as hazard" has historically been the primary focus of risk management, but it can open encouraging possibilities as well.

Risk Management, in its fullest sense, is an activity that seeks to minimize day-to-day hazards and maximize the potential returns from strategic opportunities.

There have been many attempts to define risk. The ISO defines risk as "the effect of uncertainty on objectives", where "uncertainties" are events that may or may not happen, as well as lack of information or ambiguity.

Not only can actual events affect outcomes of our objectives, but the information about the events is almost equally important. We may have to deal with information about an event that never happened, as well as with ambiguous or distorted information about actual event.

Contents

Abbreviations

A full explanation of the terms is given in Chapter 10, Glossary.

ABS	Asset Backed securities	FI	Financial Institution
A-IRB	Advanced-Internal Rating Based Approach	F-IRBA	Foundation-Internal Rating Based Approach
ALM	Asset-Liability Management	FPC	Financial Policy Committee
AMA	Advanced Measurement Approach	FSA	Financial Services Authority
BaU	Business as Usual	HUD	Department of Housing and Urban Development
BIA	Basic Indicator Approach		
BIPRU	The Prudential Source Book for Banks, Building Societies and Investment Firms Instrument	ICAAP	Internal Capital Adequacy Assessment Process
		IM	Internal Model
		IMA	Internal Model Approach
CAR	Capital Adequacy Ratio	ISP	Information Systems Professional of Canada
CDO	Collateralised Debt Obligations		
		ITCP	Information Technology Certified Professional aligned with the International Professional Practice Partnership
CMA	Certified Management Accountant (Canada)		
CRD	Capital Requirements Directive		
		MBS	Mortgage-Backed Securities
EAD	Exposure at Default		
ELC	Entity Level Controls	MCR	Minimum Capital Requirement
ERM	Enterprise Risk Management		
		NSFR	Net Stable Funding Ratio
EU	European Union	ORSA	Own Risk and Solvency Assessment
EUR	Euro		
FCA	Financial Conduct Authority	OTC	Over-the-counter

PCAOB	Public Company Accounting Oversight Board	ROCA	Return on Capital Allocated
PD	Probability of Default	RTS	Report to Supervisor
PILLAR2/ICAAP	Internal Capital Adequacy Assessment Process	SCR	Solvency Capital Requirement
		SEC	US Securities and Exchange Commission
PRA	Prudential Regulation Authority	SFCR	Solvency and Financial Condition report
PSB	Prudential Source Book	SOX	Sarbanes-Oxley
QRT	Quantitative Reporting Templates	TSA	The Standard Approach
RAROC	Risk Adjusted Rate of Return	VaR	Value at Risk

Chapter 1,
The labyrinth of risks in financial institutions

The authors of this book imagine they are having a discussion with Luca Pacioli. Pacioli (1445-1517) was an Italian mathematician who outlined and described the system of double entry book-keeping which is still in use today. In their answers, the authors provide a summary of the chapter that follows.

Question 1

Luca Pacioli:

I understand that there are different definitions of the term "risk"; can you explain the key ones to me?

We reply:

o   There are different types of losses: expected and unexpected. Expected losses are changes in values that can be derived from information currently anticipated, while unexpected losses are potential deviations from the expected losses or gains.

o   Risk can be defined in terms of the totality of expected and unexpected losses. Expected losses are changes in values that can be derived from information currently anticipated, while unexpected losses are potential deviations from the expected losses or gains.

o   The successful delivery of an organization's objectives is impacted by the inherent uncertainty of the business environment. This risk can be conceived as both hazard and opportunity.

Question 2

Luca Pacioli:

I understand that there are different types of financial institutions. Can you detail the primary ones to me?

We reply:

o   Risks in financial institutions are like a labyrinth consisting of many paths, such as the numerous types of organizations and risks or exposures.

o   A financial institution is an organization that facilitates the allocation of its financial resources, by way of provision of its related products and services, to potential users.

o   There are many different types of financial institutions, resulting in different categories of inherent risk.

o   Different financial institutions have different types of assets and liabilities.

1.1   Introduction

He, who every morning plans the transactions of the day, and follows that plan, carries a thread that will guide him through a labyrinth of the most busy life.

Victor Hugo

A labyrinth is a complex structure with many intricate interconnecting components. This is the case also for the labyrinth of risks in financial institutions, which includes many components, especially in relation to the numerous types of organizations and risks or exposures.

1.2   **People and assets**

*A feast is made for laughter, and wine maketh merry; but
money answereth all things.*

Ecclesiastes 10:19

In modern market society, humans exchange between
themselves goods and services they produce via the
medium of money. Human beings need money to live
their lives. The narrator of Ecclesiastes says that money
answers all things; three thousand years ago it was just
as true as it is true today. People have to feed, clothe,
educate and entertain themselves and their families,
purchase drugs and medical services for the sick. People
labour hard to receive money. They risk their life and
limb in pursuit of money. They lie and cheat and go to
prison. They climb into stratosphere and go to the
bottom of the sea. People can spend all their money
right away on bread or diamonds or save them for
future purchases or ambitious projects. People save
money to protect themselves from such things as
possible income loss, old age survival, unanticipated
medical expenses, children and education.

The same is true of industrial corporations, insurance
companies and banks. They earn money and then spend
it for new equipments, production facilities, raw
materials and employee salaries. Part of the money is set
aside for future use. To be useful in the future money
that was set aside must retain or increase their value
over time.

To this end, money is often used for the purchase of
assets. We will define assets as objects that are not
bought for their direct use by the buyer, but rather for
their ability to retain or increase their value as expressed
in the units of money. It could be precious metals (gold,
silver or platinum), foreign currency (it makes sense to
use Mongolian tugrik to purchase US dollars and keep
your savings in US dollars), objects of art (a painting by
Picasso valued at US$ 50,000 in 1948 was sold for US$
50,000,000 in 2001) or Guaranteed Investment
Certificates at a local bank that will pay 2.0% annually

(2012) or it could be bonds, stocks or other financial instruments.

When money or other financial assets are being held for a length of time that is where we encounter the financial risk: risk of assets losing their value. In our book we will look on risk factors affecting the values of assets and will discuss their identification, measurement, prediction of magnitude and ways of mitigation. But let us at first have a brief look at money, assets and their function in society.

1.3 Money

I'd like to live as a poor man with lots of money.

Pablo Picasso

It is important to understand what money is. It has three essential functions:

- to be the medium of exchange,
- to be the unit of account or value
- to be the store of value.

As a medium of exchange, money must be universally accepted as payment for goods and services. As a unit of account, money must be used to express the relative value of goods and services and, as a store of value, money must purchase the same amount of goods and services over a long period.

Type of money	Example
Currency money *(3% of all money)*	• Bills • Coins
Commodity money	• Precious metals and stones • Natural resources (oil, coal) • Other (furs, cigarettes)
Representative money	• Receipts for commodities
Credit money *(97% of all money)*	• Created by banks through fractional reserve banking process

Figure 1 – Types of money

Money comes in different form (See Figure 1). It could be familiar to all: bills and coins (currency money); precious metals (gold, silver, platinum); energy (amounts of oil, gas or coal); minerals (iron ore, bauxites or potash). At some times in history and in certain places people used as money fur, sea shell and even cigarettes (in POW camps during WWII). People used the receipts for commodities as payment for their debt (representative money).

1.4 Assets and value

There are certain dangers associated with accumulating currency money. It has to be remembered that value of currency money made of inexpensive paper depends on trust. A little piece of paper in your hands does not have any intrinsic value without the general agreement to accept it in exchange of real goods and services. The integrity of money is guaranteed by governments. Governments work hard to insure that paper issued by them is used as a medium of exchange. A government prosecutes counterfeiters, looks after the printing of money, makes sure that there is no shortage of money across the land and demands from the citizens and companies to accept its money on the territory under its control.

Currency money is as good as the country and the government that issues it. Money issued by democratic states (such as USA, UK and the European Union) are obviously a better bet than money published by Zimbabwe or the Peoples Republic of China. Governments also enforce the use of money as a unit of account. Salaries, prices, government economic statistics are all expressed in units of local currency. The only area where government fails in is insuring that money will retain its value over time. As a store of value, currency money is less than a perfect instrument. As soon as a quantity of currency is kept over a period of time the danger of it losing its value arises. Experience teaches that left alone currency money never increases in value. The opposite is true; the longer you keep the currency, the less value it carries.

You need more and more currency to buy the same thing. In 1950 an average hot dog cost approximately 10 cents. In 1970 you could not buy one cheaper than for 1 dollar. Money can also suddenly stop being a universally acceptable medium of exchange and a unit of account. After the communist revolutionaries took over the Russian Empire they banned the use of money from 1918 to 1922. All goods and services had been rationed and distributed according to government wishes. Values of money accumulated by people suddenly become zero. It could be devalued by government fiat as happened on numerous occasions in Latin America when government exchanged 10,000 old pesos for 1 new peso. Or it could be devalued with regards to the official rate of exchange paid for foreign currency. To buy 1 US dollar in a government controlled bank, one may have to pay 100 units of local currency instead of 50. The phenomenon of inflation of prices (we will talk about it later in detail) slowly but surely erodes value of currency money. Later in our book we will talk about risk factors affecting the value of currency money.

1.5   Risk factors and value of assets

So currency money is not a good store of value. We need a device that will allow us to convert the currency money into something different, something that will keep or even grow its value. That is where financial assets are coming into play.

Financial assets have two functions: to be a source of profit and to be a store of value. The buyer expects assets to retain or even increase in value. There are six major classes of financial assets: debt (loans and mortgages), stocks, bonds, futures, options and derivatives.

The good thing about financial assets that they are traded on specialized markets and could be readily converted to currency money at a market price. There are six major asset markets: money, capital, stock, bonds, futures and derivatives (See Figure 2).

Type of asset	Example
Stock	• Company stock
Bonds	• Company • Federal • State or provincial • Municipal
Futures	• Futures • Options
Derivatives	• Derivatives
Money *(maturity < 1 year)*	• T-bills • Short-term bonds • Banking acceptances • Call loans • Re-purchase agreements • NCD cert of deposit
Capital *(maturity > 1 year)*	• Mortgages • Commercial and consumer loans • Perpetuities • G-bonds (federal, state, municipal)

Figure 2 – Financial asset markets

The value of financial assets on the market fluctuates. It can go up and down. Assets can also become worthless, their value equal to zero. Assets are constantly at risk of being devalued. The value of assets is the subject of numerous risk factors working over time. The risk factors arise during the complex interplay between market participants, government regulators and information providers.

The average citizen today participates in the financial market's activities through his bank. Banking institutions today are heavily involved in activities of all financial markets. Banks accumulate money of their depositors and invest them in numerous financial assets. By investing they expose money of their depositors to financial risk factors. The educated citizen must be aware of the risk factors their money exposed to after they deposit them into their bank accounts. As the 2008 banking crisis vividly demonstrated , contrary to the belief of the former chairman of the Federal Reserve Allan Greenspan that banks would be ardent protectors of the values of their assets, banks can easily over a period of time accumulate a lot of worthless paper and therefore could only survive by injection of trillions of taxpayer's money. But what will happen if governments refuse to bail banks out (as in case of Lehman Brothers)? Every citizen must have a clear understanding of possible dangers.

1.6 Markets, players and their roles

But what about market where assets are freely traded? What are they? What risk factors arise from organization of those markets, from the nature of market participants?

How can the structure of the market affect the future value of your assets? In every financial market there are 4 roles played by participants: buyer, seller, intermediary and facilitator (See Figure 3).

One market actor can play more than one role (for example, be buyer and seller at the same time). Buyers and sellers can act for themselves or be an agent buying and selling on behalf of somebody else. The role of facilitator implies advising buyers and sellers on their asset purchases, but it also implies the origination of assets, actual creation of valuable assets as out of the thin air. The role of the intermediaries implies the transformation of assets, creation of the new values out of old. The role of facilitator came under close scrutiny during the current (2008) financial crisis. The whole process of creation of the financial assets must be scrutinized by the intelligent citizen whose money is at stake. In this book we will discuss the creation (origination) and modification of assets in more details.

We will also try to shed light on the role of information providers to markets and public.

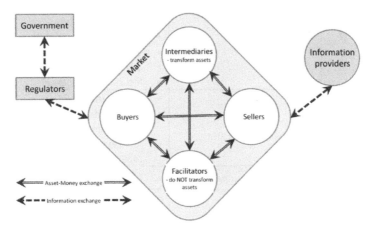

Figure 3 – Market players interaction

Among them are rating agencies, people who provide rating of assets, in effect, determining asset's price. Numerous financial newspapers, magazines, TV programmes, blogs and web sites constantly bombard public with information related to the price of assets. However, the facts they report are not always accurate or even true. The risk to the asset value they present can be illustrated by the recent activity of the 14 years-old blogger who managed to drive down price of the stock of the company he did not like by spreading false rumours about the company on his web site.

Market actors may also play roles that display blatant conflict of interest (for example rating agency serving as an adviser to an asset originator). The conflict of roles very often escapes the scrutiny not only of citizens but also market regulators appointed by governments. We will look into risk presented to the public by the movement of personnel from the government regulators into the higher echelons of management of financial institutions and vice versa (See Figure 4).

17

Type	Function (transformations)	They are:
Intermediaries	• Maturity • Risk • Convenience	• Banks • Credit unions • Building societies • Mutual funds • Brokers/financial advisers • Insurance companies
Facilitators	• Originate assets • Re-sell assets • Advice buyers and sellers	• Brokers/dealers • Underwriters of stocks and bonds • Advisers to buyers and sellers
	Compensation:	• Fees or commissions
Information providers	• Rating of assets • Analysis of asset value • News reporting • News commenting • Information distribution	• Rating agencies • Financial analysts • Business press, radio or TV • Internet bloggers • Publishers
	Compensation:	• Fees paid by buyers and sellers • Profit from publishing
Regulators	• Create and enforce rules • Protect against fraud • Prevent monopoly • Lender of last resort	• SEC (US) • Bank of England (UK) • OSFI (Canada) • OSEC (Ontario, Canada)

Figure 4 – Market players defined

1.7   Financial institutions

There are numerous financial organizations that handle your money directly or indirectly .

Most of the time the average citizen deals with the deposit taking institutions: commercial and saving banks, credit unions, savings and loans associations. That is where a citizen pay check is being deposited, financial assets of the citizen bought and sold. That is where most of the risks factors to citizen's assets values can be found.

Financial institutions

Type	Examples	Assets	Liabilities
Deposit-taking institutions	• Commercial banks • Savings banks • Credit unions • Savings and loans associations • Money market mutual funds	• Commercial loans • Consumer loans • Mortgages • Investment product	• Customer's deposits • Bank's own investment products
Finance companies	• Consumer credit companies • Automotive acceptance corporations	• Commercial loans • Consumer loans	• Company's own notes • Company's own bonds
Insurance companies	• Life insurance • Casualty and property insurance	• Commercial loans • Investment products	• Insurance policies • Own investment products
Investment companies	• Open-end mutual funds • Closed-end mutual funds • Investment banks	• Investment products	• Private funds
Exchanges	• Stock • Bond • Commodity • Currency • Futures and options		
Pension funds			

Figure 5 – Financial Institutions

In this book we will concern ourselves with the origin, identification and analysis of those factors. We will see how those factors are handled by the bank and what measures they are taking to mitigate the risks. It is the banking financial risk handling that is the main subject of this book. We will go through alternative definitions of risk, observe the risk formation events and will follow the risk control process. We will discuss models and their roles in the study of financial risks. The deposit taking institutions deal on a day-to-day basis with other financial institutions such as investment companies, exchanges and insurance companies. We will also discuss some risk factors arising from the activities of non deposit taking institutions. The reader will see how the struggle against the loss of value is being conducted and how risk control became a never ending function of the financial institutions.

1.8   Losses

There are different types of losses expected (or predictable) and unexpected (or unpredictable).

Expected losses are changes in values that can be derived from information currently anticipated, while unexpected losses are potential deviations from the expected losses or gains.

Unexpected losses arise, for example, as a result of unexpected fluctuations in market values (for example, share prices, five-year euro swap rate, five-year credit spread for Brazil), unexpected credit rating downgrades and a larger-than expected amount of loan defaults (for example, as a result of an economic crisis), or an unexpectedly high number of processing errors causing especially serious damage (for example, loan processing, payments).

1.9   What is risk?

Risks tend to focus on negative outcomes as people are afraid that negative outcome will result in not meeting their goals and objectives. Risk can also be defined as the probability and severity of assets losing its value.

Risk can broadly be defined as the things that can go wrong in a business.

More specifically, risk can be defined in terms of the totality of expected and unexpected losses.

Expected losses and unexpected losses compose the building blocks of risks. Expected losses could include:

- Expected fluctuations in market value (for example, share prices due to dividend payments; movements in bond and option prices due to changes in their residual maturity),

- Expected (average) number and amount of loan defaults and expected credit rating downgrades (rating migration),

- Expected (average) number of processing errors causing normal levels of damage.

The concept of risk involves two other concepts: the probability of occurrence of the negative outcome and the magnitude of the negative outcome. The more probable the occurrence of the negative outcome and the bigger its magnitude the higher is the risk. Taking this approach allows the measurement of risk. Probability value is simple; it runs from 0 to 1 (from total impossibility to total certainty). But magnitude is assessed in different values depending on the nature of the risk. In the financial area the magnitude of negative outcome is expressed most often in units of account (such as US dollars and euros.)

Risk is the uncertainty of an event occurring that could have an impact on the achievement of objectives (in our case, business goals such as achieving a stated return). Risk is measured in terms of both likelihood and consequences. Consequences (or impact) is a measure of the financial cost should the risk happen at all, while likelihood (or probability) is a measure of the percentage possibility of a risk happening.

1.10   The nature of risk

The successful delivery of an organization's objectives is impacted by the inherent uncertainty of the business environment. This risk can be conceived as both hazard and opportunity. 'Risk as hazard' has historically been the primary focus of risk management. This perspective emphasizes reducing the probability of a negative event without incurring excessive cost. 'Risk as opportunity' is implicit in the concept of the relationship between risk and return. The greater the risk, the greater the potential return, as well as the potential loss.

While allowing for some flexibility of focus, risk as hazard is typically related to business as usual (BaU), the day-to-day activities that serve to reduce the threats to the successful achievement of the organization's objectives. Risk as opportunity, on the other hand, is more closely related to the activities of strategic planning and management, where projects are initiated to maximize the opportunities presented by the potential upside of risk. Traditionally, managerial focus and effort has been on the prevention of hazard. Whilst this is important, in an increasingly competitive environment, this should not be to the detriment of realizing the upside opportunity that materializes through strategic initiatives and major change programs incorporated within business plans.

Risk management is considered in its fullest sense as an activity that seeks to minimize day-to-day hazards and maximize the potential returns from strategic opportunities.

1.11   Alternative definitions of risks

There have been many attempts to define risk. In 2009 The International Standards Organization created the risk standard ISO 31000:2009. In this document ISO defines risk as "the effect of uncertainty on objectives", where "uncertainties" are events that may or may not happen as well as lack of information or ambiguity. The authors want to add that it is not only actual events which can affect outcomes of our objectives, but that the information about the events is almost equally important. We may have to deal with information about an event that never happened, as well as with ambiguous or distorted information about actual event.

Risks can also be defined within the context of the applicable function. For example, credit risk is assessed based on the probability of default (likelihood) and loss given default (consequences). In operational risk, it is described as frequency (probability) and severity (impact). In both cases, risk is the possibility of an event occurring and of its resulting consequences.

Or, said another way, risk is the potential of a deviation from expectations, typically involving earnings or value.

Risk can be thought of as the uncertainty of future events, incorporating both lost opportunities as well as threats materializing, which will have an impact on the institution's ability to achieve business objectives.

It is important to understand that risk arises as much from the possibility that opportunities will not be realised as from the possibility that threats will happen.

Chapter 2,

Sleepwalking on a tightrope: Risks the players take

Question 1

Luca Pacioli:

As a man of the Renaissance, I saw much risk-taking in terms of exploration of the New World and other great leaps forward in Science and other fields of endeavour. In addition, to provide an "account" of these and other business adventures, my mathematics book titled "Everything about Arithmetic, Geometry, and Proportions" had an accounting section that served as the world's only accounting textbook until well into (I understand) the 16th century. Can you explain to me what is "risk" as a concept?

We reply:

o   Risk is both a science and an art and both are necessary components to measure and manage risk.

o   'Risk' can be conceived as both hazard and opportunity. 'Risk as hazard' has historically been the primary focus of risk management. 'Risk as opportunity' is implicit in the concept of the relationship between risk and return. The greater the risk, the greater the potential return, as well as the potential loss, and, vice versa.

o   Where something hasn't happened, and we know it, it is a "known known". We also know there are "known unknowns"; that is to say we know there are some things we do not know. But, there are also "unknown unknowns" - the ones we don't know we don't know. Risk Management has an important role in managing these different situations.

Question 2

What is "risk appetite" and "risk tolerance"?

Luca Pacioli:

We reply:

- o A firm's "Risk Appetite" is the desire to accept a specified level of risk congruent with the business and strategies for risk. "Risk Tolerance" is the amount of risk that the firm is willing to endure in order to achieve its objectives. It is always preferable for risk appetite to be less (or no more than equal to) risk tolerance.

2.1 What is risk: a science or an art?

Reports that say that something hasn't happened are always interesting to me, because as we know, there are "known knowns"; there are things we know we know. We also know there are "known unknowns"; that is to say we know there are some things we do not know. But there are also "unknown unknowns" — the ones we don't know we don't know.

Donald Rumsfeld, US Secretary of Defense (2002)

2.1.1 Measuring risk is both a science and an art

The term "risk" comes from the early Italian word *risicare* meaning dare. This is fitting in the context of the modern financial market, since risk management requires the daring to act and decide what sorts of financial activities should be done.[1] Historically, credit risk, the uncertainty on the repayment of a borrowed amount, is considered to be the oldest risk type in financial markets. Credit business rules were

---

[1]Caouette, John B. / Altman, Edward I. / Narayanan, Paul: Managing Credit Risk, New York 1998).

supposedly included in the Laws of Hammurabi dating from 1800 BC During the Renaissance, credit business was significant to Italian city states, especially in Siena and Piacenza and subsequently in Florence. The proliferation of risk based business in the Renaissance, an age of both great artists like Michelangelo and scientists like Galileo, demonstrates how both science and art are necessary components to measure and manage risk.[2]

Risk measurement comprises three fundamental questions, they are:

- Exposure: what risks and how great?

- Financial sensitivity: how will profit and loss change?

- Volatility and correlation: how large could the shocks be?

The three questions together answer the overall question: How much risk is there? This determines the assessment of how much Profits and Losses can change overall.[3]

2.2 Types of Risk

2.2.1 Risks in providing financial services

The risks associated with the provision of financial services differ according to the type of service rendered. The following table describes the risk types[4]

Risk types	Explanation
Systematic risk	Systematic risk is the risk of asset value change associated with systemic factors. As such, it can be hedged but cannot be diversified completely away. In fact, systematic risk can be thought of as undiversifiable risk. Financial institutions assume this type of risk whenever assets owned or claims

---

2 *Risk Management in Finance - Dr. Clifford Tjiok – Lehrveranstaltung - SS 2005 (presentation)*

3 *NABE Presentation, Leslie Rahl, Capital Market Risk Advisor*

4 *The Place of Risk Management in Financial Institutions by George S. Oldfield and Anthony M. Santomero, The Wharton Financial Institutions Centre 1997*

Risk types	Explanation
	issued can change in value as a result of broader economic conditions. As such, systematic risk comes in many different forms. For example, as interest rates change, different assets have somewhat differing and unpredictable value responses. Large scale weather effects can strongly influence both real and financial asset values for better or for worse. These are a few types of systematic risks associated with asset values.
	Some financial institutions decompose systematic risk more finely. Accordingly, for example, many institutions heavily involved in the fixed income market attempt to track interest rate risk closely and more rigorously than those that have little rate risk in their portfolios.
Foreign exchange risk	International investors are aware of foreign exchange risk and try to measure and restrict their exposure to it. In a similar fashion, investors with high concentrations in one commodity (for example, gold and silver) need to concern themselves with commodity price risk and perhaps overall price inflation, while investors with high single industry investments monitor both specific industry concentration risk and the forces that affect the fortunes of the industry involved.
Credit risk	Credit risk arises from non-performance by a debtor. It may arise from either an inability or an unwillingness to perform in the pre-committed contracted manner.
	Credit risk is diversifiable but difficult to hedge (that is, defend against loss) perfectly. This is because most of the default risk may in fact result from the systematic risk outlined above. The idiosyncratic nature of some portion of these losses, however, remains a problem for creditors in spite of the beneficial effect of diversification on total uncertainty. This is particularly true for creditors that lend in local markets and take on highly illiquid assets.
Counterparty risk	Counterparty risk comes from non-performance by the other party to the transaction. The non-performance may arise from a counterparty's refusal to perform for a number of reasons (for example, due to an adverse price movement of a traded asset caused by systematic factors, or from some other political or legal constraint that was not anticipated by the principals). Diversification is the major tool for controlling non-systematic counterparty risk.

Risk types	Explanation
	Counterparty risk is similar to credit risk, but it is generally considered a transient financial risk associated with trading, rather than a standard creditor default risk associated with an investment portfolio. A counterparty's failure to settle a trade can arise from many factors other than a credit problem.
Market risk	Market risk (in relation to a firm) is defined as the risk that arises from fluctuations in values of, or income from, assets or in interest or exchange rates.
Liquidity Risk	Liquidity risk is the risk that a firm, although solvent, either does not have available sufficient financial resources to enable it to meet its obligations as they fall due, or can secure such resources only at excessive cost.
Operational risk	Operational risk is associated with the failures in people, process or systems as well as external events.
Legal risks	Legal risks are endemic in financial contracting and are separate from the legal ramifications of credit, counterparty, and operational risks. New statutes, court opinions and regulations can put formerly well established transactions into contention even when all parties have previously performed adequately and are fully able to perform in the future.
	A second type of legal risk arises from the activities of an institution's management or employees. Fraud, violations of securities laws, and other actions can lead to catastrophic loss.

2.2.2   Risk: bad or good?

Though some might see risk in a subjective way, it is in fact not inherently good or bad, though it may be undesirable. There are key objective questions to measuring and managing risk and determining its desirability, for example:

- How much risk?

- Who is managing it?

- Is the return on the risk adequate?

- So what makes a risk undesirable?
    - If the risk is mispriced.
    - If the risk is misunderstood.
    - If the risk is mismanaged.
    - If the risk is unidentified.
    - If the risk is unintended.

In determining undesirability, the aspects of risk which you cannot control should be as small as possible. These uncontrollable aspects include:

- Clever, new forms of fraud.

- Major changes in the marketplace

- Surprise changes by governments/regulators.

- Unexpected changes in infrastructure.

- "Acts of God"[5]

2.2.3   Banking risks

Banking risks are defined as adverse impacts on a bank's profitability arising from a number of distinct sources of uncertainty.

In the banking universe, there is large number of risks. The different risks need careful definition to provide sound bases serving for quantitative measures of risks. As a result, risk definitions have gained precision over the years. Risk definitions serve as a starting point for both regulatory and economic treatments of risks. Therefore in regards to the definition of banking risks, risk measurement requires capturing the source of uncertainty and the magnitude of its adverse impact on profitability.[6]

2.2.4   Change risk

Unlike emerging risks, which are often driven by external forces, change risks are usually thought of as

5 NABE Presentation, Leslie Rahl, Capital Market Risk Advisor
6 Bessis, J., "Risk Management in Banking", Wiley, Chichester, 2005

resulting mostly from actions within the financial institution (FI).

This includes changes such as:

- When the strategy, system, product or service is new.

- When the product has never been offered in the market, currency or regulatory environment proposed.

- When the strategy, product or service has not been previously conducted in the manner proposed, or does include significant changes to existing strategies, products or services.

- When the product or service is aimed at a new market segment that has particular unique and different characteristics requiring special attention.

- When he product or service increases risk substantially or assumes new or multiple types of risks or regulatory requirements.

- When dormant products or services are to be re-introduced.

- When a new operating model or entity is proposed, such as strategic alliances, new exchange membership or new operating or legal entities.

Interaction of risk categories

The overlap of risks should be considered. Figure 6 shows the intersection of operational risks with other risks.

Experience shows that the overlap areas can result in major risk events occurring (for example rogue traders, market conduct, poor integration) In general, major losses occur when a number of controls, policies and procedures fail to operate properly.

Figure 6 – Interaction of risk categories

2.3   **Risk known and unknown**

Risk is an important component in human decision making. Every time we make a decision and perform an action of any kind we expect a certain outcome. On many occasions the outcome we expect does not come about. Sometimes the outcome is better than we expected, and it comes as a pleasant surprise. However the outcome could also be worse than we expected, and that is where the idea of risk comes into play.

We talk about risk when we are afraid that outcome of our actions will be worse than we expected. Some theorists believe that the idea of risk must include outcomes that are better than expected (so-called negative risk) but the authors believe that this usage of the word will only confuse the issue. After all we do not talk of death as negative life and health as negative disease. In the normal course of human life, risk always comes in conjunction with negative unexpected results of our decisions and actions.

2.3.1   Financial risk

How does the idea of risk apply to the sphere of finances?

Financial institutions and individuals buy, sell and keep assets whose value is expressed in units of currency. The probability and magnitude of the decrease in the value of an asset over time represents the risk encountered in the field of finance.

The value of an asset changes during the period of time it is held by its owner. Changes in value could be positive or negative. Positive change represents the increase in an asset value while negative change reduces the value of an asset. The decrease in asset value is a financial loss. Thus, in finance, risk is a term describing the probability of a loss as well as its magnitude.

2.3.2   Risk factors

Everybody who wants to keep an asset for a period of time is exposed to risk. Depending on numerous factors, the probability and magnitude of loss may vary. To analyse the risk is to identify and study factors affecting the probability and magnitude of loss. Factors affecting the risk of loss we will call the risk factors.

Looking ahead on the life time of an asset, some risk factors can be predicted ("known knowns", according to D. Rumsfeld) and therefore losses that they cause will be expected. We know that the value of an asset will undergo regular changes due to: dividend payment for shares, changes in their residual maturity for bonds, expected (average) number and amount of loan defaults and expected credit rating downgrades (rating migration) for loans, and expected (average) number of processing errors causing normal levels of damage for any type of asset.

However the predictable risk factors may display on occasion the unexpected changes in magnitude ("known unknowns", according to D. Rumsfeld) due to rapid fall in share prices, an unexpected credit rating downgrades or a larger-than expected amount of loan defaults (as a result, for example, of an economic crisis) or an unexpectedly high number of processing errors causing especially serious damage (for example, loan processing or payments).

There are also factors whose existence is not even suspected ("unknown unknowns", according to D. Rumsfeld). Those factors could cause the catastrophic unexpected losses. They could be: clever, new forms of fraud (see Bernard Madoff, sub-prime mortgages), major changes in the marketplace, surprise changes by governments or regulators, unexpected changes in infrastructure, wars, revolutions, earthquakes, floods and other acts of God.

Some authors call the risk factors in question "black swans". This refers to the fact that people for centuries believed that swans could be only white, until the Australian black swan was discovered. In much the same way, risk factors might not be seen to exist until they are discovered. In the financial world, mathematicians have developed sophisticated quantitative models to predict the behaviour of asset values over time. Unfortunately, unknown unknowns, or black swans, cannot be quantified as their very existence is not known in advance of the event. Mathematical models have substantial limitations as they are based on statistics computed from historical data. The past is not necessarily a good indicator of the future, but mankind has no other means to infer anything about future, so we must rely on the past[7].

This is different from predictable risk factors (or known knowns) which the authors refer to as white crows, given they are known to exist.

---

7 *The black swan theory is a metaphor that describes an event that is a surprise, has a major effect, and after the fact is often inappropriately rationalized with the benefit of hindsight. The theory was developed by Nassim Nicholas Taleb to explain: 1. - The disproportionate role of high-profile, hard-to-predict, and rare events that are beyond the realm of normal expectations in history, science, finance, and technology. 2. - The non-computability of the probability of the consequential rare events using scientific methods (owing to the very nature of small probabilities). 3. - The psychological biases that make people individually and collectively blind to uncertainty and unaware of the massive role of the rare event in historical affairs.*

2.3.3   Emerging risk – unknown risks

Emerging risks are defined as those risks that are at an early stage of becoming known or coming into being, and are expected to grow greatly in significance. Thus, an emerging risk is a new risk that has limited impact currently but has the potential to become a concern in the future. Emerging risks are usually driven from outside forces, either directly or indirectly.

There are some typical characteristics which can help identity emerging risks. This sort of risk may result from changes in the economic, social, legal, or physical environment or advances in technology. They might appear slowly and lead to long-term risk exposures. It is important to attempt to identify emerging risks since when they materialize they can have a significant impact. The identification also provides insight for senior management on what is on the horizon, thereby allowing early consideration of mitigating actions or strategic changes to response. Furthermore, it is an expectation of the regulatory or rating agency to identify emerging risks, a desire shared by companies and at more line of business levels as well. However, identification of emerging risks is difficult to do and involves a high degree of uncertainty. Therefore the link between cause and effect of risk exposures is difficult to prove.

The required mitigating action is the monitoring of the emerging risk or analysis of this potential risk.

Early identification of emerging risk can limit exposure to losses

In Figure 7 the graph show that at the beginning the emerging risk is unknown but is small (Ignorance), next there is a refusal to believe that the risk exists or that it is increasing (Denial), later there is acceptance that the risk is present and that it is becoming significant (Recognition) and, finally, there is full acknowledgement that the risk is major (Acceptance).

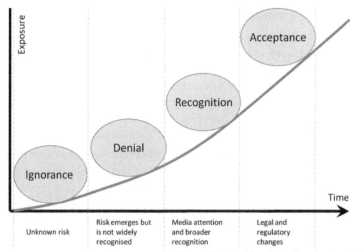

Figure 7 –Identification of emerging risks

2.4   Risk appetite and risk tolerance

2.4.1   Risk appetite

Risk appetite is a term that is frequently used throughout the risk management community, but is not always well-understood. Risk appetite, at the organisational level, is the amount of risk exposure, or potential adverse impact from an event, that the organisation is willing to accept or retain. Once the risk appetite threshold has been breached, risk management treatments and business controls are implemented to bring the exposure level back within the accepted range.[8]

Risk appetite is an expression of the level of risk the bank is willing to bear, and is expressed in its boundary statements. Or, said another way, risk appetite is the variability in results that a financial institution and its board are prepared to accept in support of the organization's business strategy. Defined clearly, risk appetite provides a framework against which all areas of the bank can make and support day-to-day and

8 *"Continuity Central" web site*

strategic business decisions. Usually risk appetite is defined in both quantitative and qualitative terms, as not all of the risks faced can be quantified. The Board should monitor its risk profile in relation to appetite on an ongoing basis using the management information provided to them. Risk appetite typically is expressed under risk appetite headings covering credit risk, market risk, operational risk and some Pillar 2 risks (for example, liquidity risks).

While there are no commonly agreed definitions, risk appetite is generally defined as the maximum amount of risk that a company is willing to accept in pursuit of its mission, objectives or plans and risk tolerance can be substituted for risk appetite for specific risk categories.

The statement of a risk appetite is an important reference point and acts as a benchmark of all risk-taking and risk mitigation activities within the organization. It provides guidance and defines boundaries, within which risk-based decision-making can occur, and provides a clear framework for the selection of one course of action over another. The risk appetite covers three broad areas: (i) the quantum of risk that the organization is comfortable assuming or retaining, (ii) the nature of the risks that the organization is prepared to assume or retain and (iii) the target level of return that the organization seeks on the risks it assumes or retains.

2.4.2   Risk tolerances

For the purpose of defining its risk appetite, the bank should define its tolerance for risk according to whether they are acceptable risks within the strategy of the firm and appropriately managed.

If those risks are undesirable and not acceptable risks within the strategy, they need to be avoided wherever possible. While recognising these undesirable risks are additional to acceptable risks, the bank should not consider these risks as pertinent to its business. As such, no limits are deemed necessary for these risks.

Risk	Explanation	Risk types included
Acceptable risks	Acceptable risks are those risks that are defined by the bank's corporate strategy and its shareholder expectations.	Credit risk, country risk, concentration risk, market risk, settlement risk, operational risk and liquidity risk.
Undesirable risks	Undesirable risks are those risks for which the bank has zero or minimal tolerance.	Reputational risk and undesirable lending activities (as defined by the bank's credit risk policy)

Connecting strategic objectives

Figure 8 – Connecting strategic objectives

Figure 8 starts with the firm's strategic objectives. The firm designs its business model to realize its goals.

The risk appetite is the amount of risk the company (that is, enterprise) is willing to take as well. Risk tolerance is the risk-taking capacity to risk appetites for specific risk types and risk-taking activities (taking into consideration risk and return trade-off, market conditions, and competitive landscape). Note: there is no definitive industry-wide consensus for the exact definitions of the various terms used within the risk appetite body of knowledge.

Tools and inputs, activities and outputs

Figure 9 shows that the starting point of the risk determination process is to consider what it trying to be achieved; that is, the outputs. This output is achieved by using the required tools and collecting the input needed.

The applicable tools include using the risk model, risk management policies, materiality limits, risk appetite statements, capital measures and the risk and control matrices.

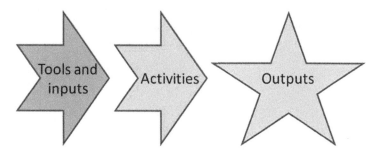

Figure 9 – Tools and inputs, activities and outputs

Using these tools, the inputs assembled include: business strategy, management's views (perspectives), key business reference information (such as business plans, process documentation and loss data), business analysis data, risk appetite details and knowledge of the existing processes/systems and controls.

With the end goal in sight (the output) and using the tools and submitting the inputs, risks appetites and tolerances are set, including a view as to the impact of current controls and improved ones on risk tolerance.

Materiality should be assessed using both quantitative and qualitative (risk) factors. Quantitative factors use total assets, net revenues or pre-tax (normalized) income as a starting point to calculate an amount. Next, qualitative factors are considered to assess if the preliminary value requires adjustment (due to events such as changing regulations, susceptibility or vulnerability to fraud, complexity of organizational structure, accounting policies, products, operations and transactions, external factors influencing the business, transaction volumes, amount of non-automated systems, use of estimates and judgment in processes).

The company should consider both the inherent and residual risks in line with the risk management methodology. Risks should be assessed in terms of both impact and probability.

2.4.3   Conclusion

If a financial institution does not fully understand its risks then its participants are taking unnecessary risks not unlike sleepwalking on a tightrope.

Chapter 3,

Calculated confidence: assessing risks

Question 1

Luca Pacioli: The concept of risk is an area that has been of interest to myself and many of my Renaissance contemporaries, such as many explorers of my time period including Christopher Columbus. So, what exactly does the term "risk analysis" entail?

We reply:
o   Risk analysis is the process that identifies, assesses and records all material inherent and residual risks. It is both a science and an art. It requires knowledge and utilization of a defined methodology and applicable tools but with skill and imagination.

Question 2

Luca Pacioli: I'm interested in understanding better how risk is measured. While some call me "Friar Luca" as well as the "Father of Accounting," I really did not invent the system. Instead, I simply described the method used by merchants in Venice during the Italian Renaissance period. For example, I did write about the use of journals and ledgers, and I warned that a person should not go to sleep at night until the debits equalled the credits! So, please tell me how is risk measured?

We reply:

- o Risk is measured in terms of both likelihood and consequences.
- o A company needs to have comprehensive policies for various individual risk types, related to the identification, analysis and measurement of the various types of risk, and management of same.

Question 3

Luca Pacioli:

Providing good stewardship and management was key in my time as well as of course in your modern times. How does Risk Management today support the Management of a business?

We reply:

- o Risk Management supports the Management through the identification, assessment, reporting and management of risk which may threaten the achievement of the firm's business objectives.

Question 4

Luca Pacioli:

I've always been interested in methods and tools of various kinds as they assist in accomplishing tasks. For example, my book "Summa de arithmetica, geometria, proportioni et proportionalita " (The Collected Knowledge of Arithmetic, Geometry, Proportion and Proportionality) was one of the early books published on the Gutenberg press. I think it is fair to say that since printing a book was an extremely expensive proposition in 1494, my book was judged to be an important enough publication to be worth the expense. Therefore, this is an area that interests me. So, what methods and tools are available to support the management of risk?

We reply:

o   Risk Indicators or "risk metrics" are information which can provide predictive insight into the financial institution's exposures.

o   Tools, models and methodologies allow for the systematic measurement and management of risk adjusted profitability and economic capital. They provide important foundation for the Enterprise Risk Management system. The use of models is an important vehicle to measure and monitor risks across the company, enhance risk management and ultimately determine capital requirements.

o   Rating agencies provide investors with assessments of the risks associated with an investment. For financial services companies, ratings by External Assessments comprise an important aspect in the evaluation of their risks.

3.1 Risk analysis and measurement: science and art

3.1.1 What is risk analysis?

Risk analysis is the process that identifies, assesses and records all material inherent and residual risks. The Risk analysis process provides a common approach to determine the nature, scale and complexity of risks, in terms of both their potential impact and probability of occurring as well as for reporting purposes.

3.1.2 Who does risk analysis?

Business management should undertake risk analysis on an ongoing basis with facilitation and challenge from the risk function, as appropriate. Formal reporting of the risk analysis process is required on a periodic basis (usually, at least quarterly).

3.1.3 How is risk analysis done?

Effective risk analysis requires a blend of quantitative and qualitative assessment. Businesses should collate a range of inputs including the goals and strategic plans of the business, as well as significant business processes and other relevant information for the analysis process. These inputs along with management experience and knowledge enable businesses to consider the threats to the achievement of business objectives.

Risk analysis should be executed in a systematic way, encompassing identification, assessment and recording of risks that could prevent the business from achieving its goals. All threats or risks identified should be reviewed in relation to the full set of inherent risks to which the business is subject, per its risk profile.

Inherent risk (sometimes called absolute risk or pure risk) is the risk before any controls or mitigating actions are put in place or the risk remaining in the case that the controls and mitigating actions in place all fail. The residual risk assessment takes into account the effectiveness of existing controls and other mitigating actions (for example transfers of risk). Moreover, control activities are assessed for their overall ability to mitigate the inherent risk to an appropriate level. Inherent risks are any issues that could prevent the business from achieving its objectives. Residual risk assessments are used for capital assessment purposes. Said another way, the key concepts are: how often an event will occur (that is, inherent risk), should occur (that is, risk appetite), and is likely to occur (residual risk). Thus, residual risk is the value of risk after taking into account any mitigating controls (that is, inherent risk minus current controls). It is also known as the risk remaining after risk treatment. Many consider residual risk to be an expression of the current risk exposure of the business, which thus indicates areas of threat and management focus. Whereas inherent risks are assessed, residual risks constitute the risk profile and are reported to management. Residual risk is the basis for any planning changes in risk mitigation, including the control environment.

The assessment stage of the risk analysis process requires consideration of the impact of future possible events and the probability of their occurrence, along with comparison of this impact to the business tolerance of loss.

The output from risk analysis should be a business risk profile, outlining the status of each risk against appetite and tolerances.

3.1.4   Why is risk analysis done?

Risk analysis helps to focus attention on material risks, as well as on responding to material risks, and further supports prioritisation of the appropriate response. A better awareness and understanding of the inherent and emerging risks which the business faces ensures a more robust approach to addressing the potential liabilities and obstacles in order to achieve the strategic objectives of the business.

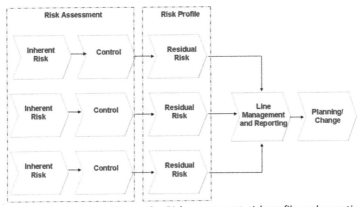

Figure 10 – Risk assessment, risk profile and reporting

Risk assessment, risk profile and reporting

Figure 10 describes the relationship between risk analysis, risk profile and reporting.

Inherent risk is the risk before any controls or mitigating actions are put in place, while residual risk takes into account the effectiveness of existing controls and other mitigating actions.

Line management has the primary responsibility for the effective identification, management, monitoring and reporting of risks to the company's management. Based on the risk assessment and determination of the risk profile, adjustments and changes can be made to plans.

People to involve in risk identification

Figure 11 starts at the top and moves in a clockwise fashion. First (at the position of just before noon) the general management team can provide an overview perspective on the area where risks are being identified and assessed.

Figure 11 – People to involve in risk identification

Next, business partners can also provide input for the identification of risks; for example, outsourcing vendors can provide details informally (through discussions) or formally (through reports with data such as metrics on volumes and losses incurred), in addition, consultants can report on both general and specific matters of concern. Senior management can also help identify risks as it has a broad high-level perspective that can review across functions (for example consider all of front office as well as the supporting middle and back offices).

Next, process specialists and owners can provide detailed knowledge of the processes being performed (for example, this could include software application support staff for a loan accounting system). Local business line management can provide an overview perspective on the area where risk are being identified and assessed; this is because they have a "close to the scene" perspective. Also, staff with risk assessment experience from other parts of the operating company can identify risks as well (for example, internal audit, compliance and finance staff can provide input to risk management on the identification of risks). This is in addition to functional experts with expert knowledge who can assist as well; for example, tax and procurement staff.

Ways of performing risk identification

Figure 12 starts at the top and moves in a clockwise fashion.

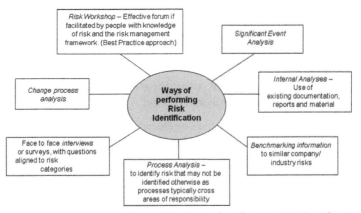

Figure 12 – Ways of performing risk identification

A risk workshop can be used, attended of course by knowledgeable people, to help determine the applicable risks present. Next, significant event analysis can be used to help identify risks; this can include a review due to a significant loss (or perhaps a near miss event) or analysis of series of systemic events. Often when a loss event occurs it is due to a series of issues or errors. Risks can also be identified by the internal analysis of existing documentation, reports or materials; this can include reports by management, consultants or auditors. Face to face interviews with knowledgeable staff can provide details on risks given the vast knowledge, experience and skills of these staff members. Similar to internal analyses, change process analysis can provide information on risks including the introduction of new risks or negation or reduction of old risks; for example, the move from a manual to a computerised system adds additional processing type risks.

Risk identification

Risk identification requires consideration of the following:

- Does the business have any specific objectives or deliverables that affect the firm's strategic objectives?

- Are there any issues that could prevent the business from achieving its objectives?

- Over the last few years, what problems have affected the business?

- What could potentially stop the firm from achieving its performance criteria?

- What problems or changes can we see in the future that may affect our business achieving its objectives?

- What issues are the firm's competitors facing and is the company likely to be affected in a similar way?

- What are the significant risks associated with the firm's business processes?

- Are there any business opportunities that the company is missing?

Supporting documentation useful for risk identification

Different types of information provide details for risk identification purposes. Business plans provide details on the business model and how management intends to operate the business (including factors such as business lines, products and geographic markets). Internal audit reports provide an independent assessment of the business including, for example, an opinion on the accuracy of the books of account and efficiency and effectiveness of operations, as well as identification of weakness found in internal controls and policy compliance. Control and risk self-assessments details the view of management on the adequacy (design) and effectiveness (compliance) of controls and whether risks are properly mitigated and control objectives met. Complaints data can often identify weaknesses in the controls that deliver products or services to customers (sometimes related goodwill payments provide a financial measure as well). Loss event information (both actual and near misses) provide information on the root causes of the loss; given their financial impact it is important to address the causes. Compliance data details help identify regulatory and related risks. Third party consultant's reports can also provide information on risks and exposures.

Documentation which may be useful for risk identification	
• Business Plans • Internal Audit Reports • Control and Risk Self Assessments • Complaints data	• Loss Events Information • Compliance data • Third Party Consultant Reports • Health and safety data

Risk analysis example

The steps in the following table detail an example of the execution of a risk analysis.

Risks are identified by first understanding the company's Business Model and locating the threats to the firm's achievement of its business objectives. The identified threats are mapped to the company's Risk Model to ensure the listing of risk exposures is complete.

Next, the risks are assessed. The first part is to assess risks as to their significance on an inherent basis (that is, before the impact of risk mitigants is considered). Next, the importance of risks is considered based on the after-impact effect of mitigants (such as internal controls); this assessment should consider the risks. Risks, both inherent and residual, are then compared to risk appetite/tolerance.

All of the above is recorded in the risk profile which, of course, is subject to change.

Risk analysis example: steps in the process		
Step 1	Identify the risk	• Identify the threats to firm's achievement of business objectives • Map the threats identified to the company's Risk Model.
Step 2	Assess the risk	• From an inherent risk perspective • From a residual risk perspective (considering financial, operational and reputational criteria). Include quantitative assessment, as required • Evaluate the risk against appetite or tolerance.
Step 3	Record the business risk profile.	

3.2   Who does risk management?

We will now discuss the related, but differing, concepts of risk and crisis. Let's start by defining these two concepts.

Risk is the uncertainty of an event occurring that could have an impact on the achievement of objectives; in our case, business goals (such as earning a reasonable profit and/or return on investment).

A crisis is the manifestation of an uncertain future event which is assumed to result in a loss (immediately or in the future).

We will now compare and contrast these two concepts in greater detail.

How to measure risk?

Figure 13 shows that risk is the product of impact times probability. The impact and probability of each risk should be assessed on both an inherent basis (before any controls or mitigating actions are put in place or the risk that the controls and mitigating actions in place all fail) and a residual basis (taking into account controls identified and their effectiveness, and other mitigating actions) basis.

Figure 13 – How to measure risk

Impact is a measure of the financial cost should the risk happen at all. Severity or impact is the consequence or outcome of a risk. Impact is usually measured in monetary terms.

Probability is a measure of the percentage likelihood of a risk happening at all. Probability or likelihood is the extent to which an event is likely to occur.

Residual risk is the likely impact and probability of a risk, after taking into account the controls and mitigations in place that have been designed to mitigate the risk to an acceptable level in line with the risk appetite of the business. In this case, you assess the probability and impact of a risk, taking into account the existence (that is, adequacy) and effectiveness of the controls and other mitigating actions identified.

Risk is measured in terms of both consequences and likelihood. Risk is all about the uncertainty of future events and how they have an impact on the ability of the firm to achieve its objectives.

3.2.2   Impact of risk

Sometimes a risk results in a loss to the organization. This can include events such as uncollectable loans, reduction in value of an asset, unexpected required legal payments, regulatory fines and customer re-imbursements (that is, events with a profit and loss impact only).

In some cases, a risk does not result in a direct and immediate financial loss but has a potential to do so. For example, an institution's reputation could be hurt by an event and this may result in a loss of future profitability.

3.2.3 Necessary conditions for risk

Risk has two necessary conditions:

- Exposure – Something about which we care about or something of interest to us.

- Uncertainty.

Frank Knight (an American economist who spent most of his career at the University of Chicago, where he became one of the founders of the "Chicago School") gave a famous definition of risk: "risk relates to objective probabilities while uncertainty relates to subjective probabilities". However, this definition is somewhat problematic since according to common usage, risk entails both uncertainty and exposure.

Harry Markowitz (American economist and a recipient of the John von Neumann Theory Prize and the Nobel Memorial Prize in Economic Sciences.) does not define risk per se, but, instead constructed the following rule: ".. that the investor does (or should) consider expected return a desirable thing and variance of the return an undesirable thing."

Risk then is exposure to a proposition of which one is uncertain.[9]

Risk analysis and risk management

Figure 14 describes how risk analysis is the systematic use of information (which may include information such as historical data and informed opinions) to

---

9 *"Defining Risk" by Glyn A. Holton, Financial Analyst Journal, Volume 60, Number 6, 2004 – CFA Institute*

estimate the probability and impact of identified risks. It provides a basis for risk evaluation, risk treatment and risk acceptance.

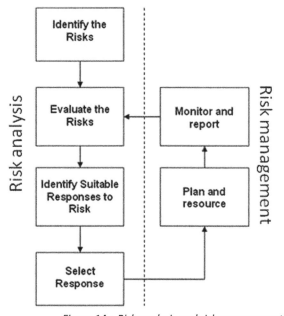

Figure 14 – Risk analysis and risk management

Risk assessment is the identification and analysis of relevant risks to the achievement of the objectives, forming a basis for determining how the risks should be managed. Because economic, industry, regulatory and operating conditions will continue to change, mechanisms are needed to identify and deal with the special risks associated with change.

Risk monitoring (after selecting the appropriate response) is the monitoring of progress of actions to implement risk management decisions (particularly those reducing residual risk so as to align to target risk).

3.2.4   Risk appetite and risk tolerance

There is no industry-wide consensus for the exact definitions of the terms risk appetite or risk tolerance. Therefore, the authors suggest the following:

A firm's risk appetite is the desire to accept a specified level of risk congruent with the business and risk strategies.

Risk Tolerance is the amount of risk that the firm is willing to endure in order to achieve its objectives.

Important benchmarks are:

- If a firm's appetite to risk is greater than its tolerance to risk a dangerous situation exists.

- It is always preferable for risk appetite to be less (or no more than equal to) risk tolerance.

A key role of Risk Management is to adjust risk appetite to risk tolerance.

3.3   Assigning the rating to assets

Credit Rating agencies provide investors with assessments of the risks associated with an investment.

In all of the cases, the key element is an assessment of risk or exposure. This includes assessing many different areas such as financial, management and currency.

For financial services companies, ratings by external assessments comprise an important aspect in the evaluation of credit risk, country risk and market risk, as well as in its risk management, risk weightings, capital adequacy computations and in meeting regulatory requirements. These ratings are a tool in the risk management process for the evaluation, comparison, monitoring and controlling of the bank's or insurer's risk with a focus on exposures and uncertainty.

Credit rating agency's term	Explanation
Debt rating	A "debt rating" is essentially an alternative term for credit rating.
Bond rating	A "bond rating" is the rating of the risk of a debt instrument of an issuer. The focus, of course, is on the ability of the issuer to meet interest and principal payments as scheduled.
Sovereign debt rating	A "sovereign debt rating" is an assessment of a country's ability to pay its debt obligation as required.
Rating agency downgrade	A "rating agency downgrade" limits the company's ability to issue debt, equity or hybrid instruments for sale to the public.
Rating agency upgrade	A "rating agency upgrade" improves the company's ability to issue debt, equity or hybrid instruments for sale to the public.

3.4 Risk indicators

Key Risk Indicators (KRIs) or risk metrics are statistics (often financial in nature) which can provide predictive insight into the financial institution's exposures. These indicators should be reviewed on a periodic basis to alert the firm to changes that may be indicative of emerging risks or deterioration of internal control. To qualify for the advanced approach to calculate operational risk capital under the Basel II requirements, regulators require banks to have a robust process in place to identify, measure, monitor and control risk. Identifying and tracking risk metrics are essential components of this process and therefore are a key component in the management of operational risk. KRIs are forward-looking risk drivers and can be predictive of future operational losses. KRIs should be tracked against pre-established thresholds as a measure of the internal control effectiveness. Examples of KRIs in trading include failed trades, unmatched trades and failed payments.

Indicators: a simple explanation

Figure 15 describes how a KRI assesses the possibility and magnitude (or impact or severity) of the risk occurring, including any changes from the prior assessment through the risk and control assessment process.

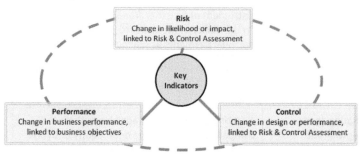

Figure 15 – KRIs: a simple explanation

A Key Control Indicator provides insight on the design (that is, its adequacy) of an internal control and how it performs or complies (that is, its effectiveness) to company policy.

A Key Performance Indicator measures business performance and is linked to the meeting of business objectives; it can include financial measures, like return on equity, and non-financial, such as market share.

3.4.2 Why are KRIs useful?

KRIs are measurable values that are a means of monitoring changes in risks and causes.

By monitoring them, the firm can identify changing risk exposures, for example a percentage increase in staff turnover in a business unit's call centres may result in an increased risk of "inadequate service delivery to customers" or goodwill payments.

KRIs support the management of risk as an early warning system of potential movements in risk.

3.4.3　Selecting KRIs

The KRIs chosen will depend both on what are the most appropriate indicators for the risk and likely causes, as well as data available (that is the correct management information). The KRI should be such that:

- It can be specifically measured, that is a KRI such as a figure, a percentage or a rating.

- Each KRI has a pre-defined limit, which will trigger a reassessment of the risk. If the limits are too tight it will always be flagged, but if too loose it will never trigger.

- Some KRIs can be built around existing Key Performance Indicators (KPIs) and as such have a dual purpose.

Different risks may require a variety of KRIs. Often, you made need two to four KRIs for each significant risk.

Which Indicators are key?

In determining what should be classified as a key indicator, there is a need to look at the risk assessment as well as information flows. The opinions of users should be considered, to find out which indicators are currently key for them. Existing indicators should be analysed, but it is important to note that key indicators change over time. It is important to note that an automated solution is always preferable to achieve cost-effectiveness.

3.4.4　Uses and benefits of indicators

The following are uses and benefits of indicators:

- Track changes.

- Analyse trends and anticipate losses.

- Challenge risk and control assessments.

- Monitor performance against risk appetite.

- Model risks, controls and losses.

- Allow the business to set realistic and achievable improvement targets.

- Target finite resources on those areas which will provide the business with most benefit.

3.5   Tools and models

3.5.1   Primary components of an ERM programme

There are two main aspects of an Enterprise Risk Management (ERM) framework or programme.

Tools, models and methodologies

Risk tools

The first is focused on developing the tools, models and methodologies to allow for the systematic measurement and management of risk adjusted profitability and economic capital. A fully embedded ERM will incorporate:

- Processes to ensure decisions such as business planning and product design are based upon maximising the return on economic profit; subject to:

- Risk appetite constraints; articulated via:

- Risk limits and thresholds; supported by:

- Economic capital quantification and allocation, and

- Risk adjusted performance monitoring and reporting by business, as well as:

- Processes to measure, oversee and manage risk exposures.

Risk culture

Responsibilities

The second aspect focuses on risk culture: the behaviours and capabilities of a bank's people. There is a need to develop formal communications and an engagement framework to continue to reinforce the awareness of members of staff to their responsibilities. Senior management should continue to reinforce strong ethical standards and to include relevant risk management objectives in their personal objectives.

Risk culture is actively supported by the risk management function (for example, credit, market and operational risks) and is responsible for:

- Developing strategies to identify, assess, monitor and control or mitigate risk.

- Codifying firm-level policies and procedures concerning risk management and controls.

- The design and implementation of the firm's risk management assessment methodologies.

- The design and implementation of risk-reporting systems for risk management.

3.5.2 Policies, procedures and standards

The board of directors of the firm is required to provide supervision and governance to the risk procedures. All risk management methodologies and models must be approved by the board, including all significant changes. All key risk management policies and procedures must be documented and authorized by the board and they should be updated annually. The bank should have comprehensive policies for risk management, related to identification and measurement of the various types of risk, and to the establishment of limits within which a bank manages its overall exposures.

In the Basel II accord (used by banking), advanced models are being used (credit risk, market risk and operational risk) and institutions must ensure that the models they are using are supported by risk management systems that are conceptually sound and implemented with integrity.

These qualitative criteria of Basel II require that the board reviews capital results from its risk management systems. Further, the institution's internal risk measurement models must be closely integrated into the day-to-day risk management processes of the institution. The risk measurement systems should be used in conjunction with the limits. The limits used should be related to the institution's risk measurement models in a manner that is consistent over time and that is well understood by both line management and senior management. In addition, institutions should have a routine in place for ensuring compliance with a documented set of internal policies, controls and procedures concerning the risk measurement systems. Finally in developing models in-house, a series of validation standards must be designed and utilized to ensure the firm meets the regulatory requirements.

Three Pillar Approach	
Pillar 1	Quantitative Requirements: How much capital an insurer should hold
Pillar 2	Requirements for the governance and risk management of insurers. Also, capital is "add-on" (that is, increased) when assessed as necessary.
Pillar 3	Supervisory reporting and transparency requirements
	Key Risks in Solvency II that are unique for Insurers
	• Underwriting Risk Risk that claims are higher than expected; caused by external or internal factors
	• Actuarial Risk Risk that actuarial assumptions are wrong (mainly Life related or longer term policies)
	• Claims Risk Risk that claims are mismanaged

Similar to the Basel II accord, in the Solvency II Accord (used in EU countries and Israel), advanced models are being used for the key insurance risks as well as other risks (such as credit risk, market risk, operational risk). Institutions must ensure that the models they are using are supported by risk management systems that are conceptually sound and implemented with integrity. In order to achieve this, they need to meet the requirements of Solvency II's Three Pillar Approach.

3.5.3   Three lines of defence

The 'three lines of defence' model encourages close working relationships between line management and the local risk function whilst facilitating independent assurance by internal audit.

3-lines model

		Description
FIRST	Business management	Responsible for the managing of risk and the application of controls.
SECOND	Risk management	Provide assurance to the Executive, Risk-related Committees and Board on the effectiveness of risk management across all risk areas of the company.
		Ongoing monitoring of risk profile and exposure.
		Aggregate and analyse risk exposure at various levels of the organization, across all risk categories. • Support for and challenge on the completeness and accuracy of risk assessments, risk reporting and the adequacy of mitigation plans
		Determine appropriate action for unacceptable risk exposure, including divestment and hedging, etc.
		Challenge management's assessment of risk and adequacy of plans to mitigate unacceptable risk.
		Develop and maintain integrated risk management framework. • Developing a Risk Management Framework to ensure it remains fit for purpose, the business is focused on material inherent risks and appetite is suitably calibrated
		Develop and deliver risk management information. • Challenge to, and the development of, MI linked to strategic planning, the Budgeting and Reporting process, capital allocation and providing assurance that residual risks remain within risk appetite.

		Description
		Provide training to reinforce awareness and support embedding.
		Additionally: • Risk managers need to have a clear understanding of the business. • Risk managers need timely, accurate data, as well as the authority to enforce actions and impose rapid sanctioning mechanisms when appropriate. Roles and responsibilities must be clearly allocated. • The effectiveness of the second line of defence requires that the control functions (finance, risk, compliance) work hand in hand.
THIRD	Group audit	Responsible for providing independent and objective assurance on the robustness and application of the Risk Management Framework and the appropriateness and effectiveness of internal controls.

The three lines of defence model is operated in a way that primary responsibility for risk identification and management lies with business management who are thus the first line of defence. Specialist risk functions are the second line of defence, as they provide support for and challenge of the completeness and accuracy of risk assessments, as well as risk reporting and adequacy of mitigation plans. The third line of defence is the internal audit, which provides independent and objective assurance on the robustness of the risk management framework and the appropriateness and effectiveness of internal control.

3.5.4 Management and risk management

Overall, risk management supports management through identification, assessment, reporting and management of risk which may threaten achievement of the firms' business objectives. Risks associated with strategic projects and change initiatives should be adequately identified and managed.

To assist the firm in managing risks, risk management has certain responsibilities. Risk management must maintain the integrity of the risk management framework (including the approach to managing risk). Risk management also must maintain the integrity of the risk management policy set and supporting guidance material for the risk management framework. Risk managers are responsible for acting in an advisory capacity to set the risk appetite and provide guidance on establishing the control environment to ensure risks are managed within appetite. Risk managers should provide advice, support and technical guidance in relation to the policy. Further, they should define the management information required from the business for the supervisory committees (both management and board) to discharge their governance supervision and also provide technical advice and reports to these committees as appropriate. They are responsible for the methodology (including direction on economic capital tools) and for the quantification of risk for risk-based capital management within the firm. Quantification may sometimes be based on subjective quantification (or qualitative methodologies) when hard data is not available in order for operational failure and reputation impact to form part of the analysis.

Types of Models

The Risk Model is the firm's representation of the risk management processes to support management of the business, including articulation of the overall risk profile of the business and to calculate the capital requirements. The risk model is the overarching environment that incorporates the risk and capital model and associated processes for the identification, assessment, measurement, managing, monitoring and reporting of risks.

The Control Model is the framework in which the risks, control objective, internal controls and the control assessment process are applied. The control model's assessment component assesses the control activities ability to mitigate the levels of inherent risk to an appropriate level. The control's ability to mitigate a risk is assessed in terms of the adequacy of the control design and the effectiveness of implementation and operation of that control. Internal controls tend to be the primary way of managing risks.

	What is this?	**What value does it offer?**
Risk model	A model of risk categories or 'risk buckets' that directs people to consider all risks that threaten delivery of the organization's objectives.	• Informs strategy and business plans • Prioritises management activity on addressing threats to delivering objectives • Supports completeness reporting
Control model	A model of control categories that provides minimum standards to be applied to keep business activity or the operating environment within what is expected or acceptable.	• Ensures business processes operate as planned • Directs managers to allocate resources effectively • Distinguishes between process controls and controls for risk mitigation • Directs audit plans.
Process model	A model of business processes executed by people and systems in order to deliver products/services to internal or external customers.	• Identifies opportunities for efficiencies (bottlenecks, duplication) • Forces 'customer' orientation • Process-based MI informs decision making.

The Process Model is the end-to-end process workstream for a transaction or activity that contributes to risk for the firm. The type of risk arising from the reduction or removal of controls, with the potential to cause uncertainty as to the achievement of business objectives or maintenance of key processes is sometimes called process risk. The core business processes are the fundamental operational processes within the business.

Risk Appetite is a tool to help managers with their decision-making

The objective is to remain within acceptable risk tolerance and, thus, optimise the risk/reward position. To do this, the manager in the business must clearly understand how much risk is acceptable (See Figure 16).

The risk-return trade-off means that the potential return rises with an increase in risk, with the opposite true as well. Or said another way, low levels of uncertainty (low risk and, thus, less capital required) are associated with lower potential returns whereas high levels of uncertainty (high risk, and thus, more capital required) are associated with higher potential returns. The risk-based risk and capital management framework measures the company's level of risk and the amount of capital that is required to support the applicable risk profile adequately and, therefore, incorporates the concept of risks versus returns.

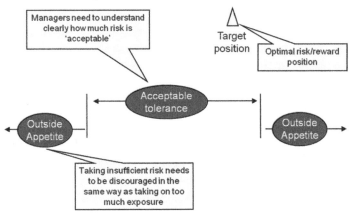

Figure 16 – Understanding Risk Appetite

3.5.5   Conclusion

The assessment of risk is both science and art. While management is required to manage the risk, the risk function has a key partnership role as well. The three lines of defence model support this. This is especially true for risk management which acts as an independent second level of control function providing first line management with an independent view of the company's risks and to support mitigation efforts on those exposures.

Chapter 4,

Getting it just right: public supervision of risk

Luca Pacioli:

I spent most of my life in Italy and as you may know, the role of the state was very small when I lived there. In fact, the church executed many of the roles that government does today such as education and operating hospitals. For this and other reasons I, in fact, became a monk and dedicated my life to God. It was at the Pope's suggestion that I took the vows of Franciscan Minor. Therefore, I'm very interested in understanding what us the role of government (or similar) organisations in their supervisory role of financial institutions in a modern 21st century democratic-capitalist society?

We reply:

○ Government organizations establish risk standards and have two major goals. The first is to set and enforce reasonable standards so that individual banks and insurance companies prudently manage their risks. The second is to ensure the resiliency of the overall banking and insurance systems.

○ Banks and insurers are government licensed institutions. As a result, the banking and insurance regulators provide extensive supervision over financial institutions and their activities. Regarding risk globally, the most important regulations for banking come from Basel II, while for insurance in the European Union it is the Solvency II Directive.

Question 2

Luca Pacioli:

I know of a small city in Switzerland by the name of "Basel" and the word "solvency" means "able to pay all debts", but the terms "Basel II" and "Solvency II" seems strange to me. Can you tell me what they are?

We reply:

o   Both the Basel II Accord and the Solvency II Directive are regulations with similar aims, which are to create a prudential framework and standards of governance more appropriate to the true risks facing the respective organizations and to establish incentives for companies to understand and manage their own risks better. They both have three pillars for Risk and Capital measurement.

Question 3

Luca Pacioli:

What do you mean by the term "standards of governance" and how is it different from the similar term of "corporate governance"?

We reply:

o   Standards of governance provide the foundation by which firms are directed and controlled. Corporate Governance is concerned with the relationships and responsibilities between the board, management, shareholders and other relevant stakeholders within a legal and regulatory framework.

Luca Pacioli:

I understand that a country in the new world, I think it is called the "United States of America" has some rules written by two of its lawmakers that establish accounting type rules. In my time the new world was just being discovered by Christopher Columbus. In fact, I wrote my seminal book on book-keeping and other related mathematical topics in 1494 which was only two years after Christopher Columbus made his first voyage to America. The name of my publication was "Summa de Arithemetica, Geometria, Proportioni et Proportionalita". As this is very close to my original book of work, can you tell me what these new accounting rules are about?

We reply:

o   In the United States, the Sarbanes-Oxley Act requires management to perform an assessment of its internal controls over financial reporting and to provide a written report detailing the effectiveness of those internal controls.

4.1   Public organizations establish risk standards

The governmental authorities have two major goals. The first is to set and enforce reasonable standards so that individual banks (and insurance companies) prudently manage their risks. The second is to ensure the resilience of the overall banking and insurance systems. Their goals do not include the prevention of bank failures at all cost, nor to save every failed bank or collapsed insurer. Therefore, banking and insurance supervision is a balancing act: it must not be too tight or too lax. It must be in accordance with the "Goldilocks and the Three Bears" "just right" principle (applicable to both porridge and regulatory supervision). However, financial institutions' supervision should also be efficient to minimize the burden imposed on banks.

4.2 National and international supervision of risk

Banks and insurers are government licensed institutions. As a result, the banking and insurance regulators provide extensive supervision over financial institutions and their activities. Regarding risk globally, the most important regulations for banking come from Basel II, while for insurance in the European Union it is the upcoming Solvency II Directive.

4.2.1 Who is watching the gamblers?

Why are banks and insurers regulated by public authorities?

The governmental banking and insurance authorities use a public safety net approach to protect those such as depositors and insurance policy holders, in the view that this benefits society. Certain tools are used in regulation, including deposit insurance, lender of last resort (provides funds when no alternatives are available) and implicit certification of soundness (good financial health) including capital requirements.[10]

4.2.2 National and international banking authorities

An essential element of a bank's or an insurer's regulatory compliance is the establishment of an effective risk management framework in order to comply with the required regulations. One such regulation is the Basel II Accord, which refers to the BIS/Basel Committee on Banking Supervision's "International Convergence of Capital Measurement and Capital Standards" (compilation of June 2004 Basel II Framework, issued in June 2006).

In the European Union, the Financial Services Authority (FSA) was the UK regulatory authority. The FSA

---

10 *A presentation to the "Bangko Sentral ng Pilipinas" (21 January 2005).*

published a text entitled The Prudential Source Book for Banks, Building Societies and Investment Firms Instrument (or BIPRU).

Starting in early 2013, the new UK regulatory authority is as follows:

Regulatory Entity	Responsibilities
Financial Policy Committee (FPC)	FPC in the Bank of England, to be responsible for macro-prudential regulation.
Prudential Regulation Authority (PRA)	PRA, a subsidiary of the Bank of England, responsible for micro-prudential regulation.
Financial Conduct Authority (FCA)	FCA, an independent authority, is responsible for conduct regulation. Previously, the FCA had been tentatively named the consumer protection and markets authority (CPMA).

Many banks follow Basel II, and also in the case of the UK, related regulations are recited in the Capital Requirements Directive (CRD) and the FSA Prudential Source Book (PSB). Basel II is implemented in the European Union under the authority of the Capital Requirements Directive, for which the FSA is the regulatory authority. For specified insurance companies in Europe this currently means the current Solvency I requirements and preparing for the Solvency II Directive.

4.2.3 What the authorities will require from banks and insurers

Banking supervision is a balancing act: regulation must be just right in order to ensure individual and overall efficiency of financial institutions. Risk-based supervision as demonstrated by Basel II and Solvency II is a philosophy for regulation which minimizes the burden imposed on enterprises. Supervision based upon risk allows banks and insurers to take risks so long as these financial institutions demonstrate the ability to manage and price for those risks. It also treats banks and insurers differently depending on each institution's demonstrated ability to manage risks. It does not penalize well-managed banks by making them operate under standards designed to keep weak, poorly managed banks solvent. However, it should be remembered that the public safety net can become very costly to the state and to the taxpayer.[11]

4.2.4 Banks and Insurers and the challenge of regulation

Banks and insurers must provide good corporate governance in order to meet the challenge of regulation (economic and regulatory capital). This includes the need for effective risk management and provides context for the importance of Basel II and the upcoming Solvency II.[12]

In banking, Pillars 1 and 2 of Basel II provide underlying principles for banks to follow. According to Pillar 1, banks should have capital appropriate for their risk-taking activities. In Pillar 2, banks should be able to properly assess the risk they are taking, and supervisors should be able to evaluate the soundness of these assessments. This approach is similar to that of Solvency II.

4.2.5 The need for capital in banks and insurance companies

Capital is an important consideration for banks and insurance companies, especially in regards to risk. Capital is very useful in that it forces owners to pay attention to the business and the amount of risk they are taking. The riskier the bank, the more capital should be held since capital serves as a financial buffer to enable a bank or insurer to ride out losses.

---

11 *ibid.*
12 *ibid.*

However since capital is costly, banks or insurers may choose a level of capital not commensurate to their risk profile. Thus, in some cases, a minimum capital level requirement is not enough. The Capital Adequacy Ratio (CAR) regulation particularly addresses this prudential concern. Banks are also classified into categories for supervision depending on the magnitude of their ratios. Thus, CARs are very important in risk-based supervision.

In banking, risk-based capital ratio is equivalent to Capital *divided by* Risk-weighted Assets.

CAR is a very good indicator of bank financial strength and is a sound basis for early supervisory intervention which is important in crisis prevention. CAR can be a fair and transparent criterion for granting authorities, but it must be accurately measured in order to be useful.

4.2.6 Other regulations

In addition to the ones already mentioned, other regulations are in place in pursuit of the just right amount of public supervision of risk. For example, Sarbanes-Oxley (SOX) is applicable to not just banks and insurer. SOX is an important component of the corporate governance program of most large financial institutions. Its reach extends all over the world, far beyond the United States, where it was written.

4.2.7 Comparing regulatory, economic and physical capital

Regulatory capital is the amount calculated per the required regulatory scheme.

Economic capital is used to measure the default risk, country risk and settlement risk elements of credit risk, as well as market risk and operational risk. It is also used to measure profitability and capital efficiency across the entity. Economic capital is used to absorb any losses arising from risks assumed within the bank's business and provides a measure of the amount of equity capital needed at any one time to absorb unexpected losses.

Physical capital is the amount as currently recorded in the books of account.

A capital assessment should assess the firm's entire risk profile, considering institution-specific characteristics and uncertainties, and explain any material differences between economic capital and regulatory capital. Additionally, there should be a three-way reconciliation of (1) regulatory capital, (2) economic (or risk) capital and (3) physical capital.

The Challenge: it is difficult for a single measure of risk capital to accommodate these different purposes.

4.3   Basel and Solvency

4.3.1   Basel II for banking

 Under Basel I (1988), capital was to be calculated based on a prescribed formula using risk-weighted assets. With the introduction of the market risk amendment to Basel I in 1996, regulatory capital was extended explicitly to market risk. Officially known as Amendment to the Capital Accord to incorporate Market Risks the objective of this enhancement was to provide an explicit capital charge for the price risks to which banks are exposed, particularly those arising from their trading book. The Basel Committee introduced measures whereby trading positions in bonds, equities, foreign exchange and commodities were removed from the credit risk framework and were given explicit capital charges related to the bank's open position in each instrument. Thus, regulatory capital was extended explicitly to market risk with this amendment. The Basel Committee defined two approaches for assessing market risk capital charges, namely: Standardised Approach and Proprietary or Internal Models Approach.[13]

---

13 *Risk Management in Banking, Peter Plochan, Thesis, 2007.*

In Basel II, total capital is the aggregate of the capital for Pillars 1 and 2, which includes a number of risk categories, plus "other capital" if considered necessary less any diversification benefits if applicable. Basel II's Pillar 1 capital amounts include credit, market and operational risks. Using mathematical modelling techniques, the firm may take account of risk diversification (where valid) represented by correlations between the three main risk classes in Pillar 1. There is no diversification benefits for Pillar 2, which is simply an add on.

The capital ratio concept in Basel II is essentially the same, with an unchanged numerator and a matching overall 8% minimum capital requirement (or greater based on the requirements of the banking authority for the applicable political jurisdiction). One of the main differences introduced in Basel II is that there are new ways of calculating risk weighted assets.

As noted, there are optional methods of measuring risk and, generally, using the more sophisticated (and precise) methods reduces the denominator and hence the amount of capital required to maintain the required level at, for example, 8%.

For Pillar 1, in many jurisdictions, Basel II requires banks to have capital (per required tier groupings) of at least 8% of risk-weighted assets. This includes:

- Total risk-weighted assets for credit risk (total risk-weighted assets for credit risk = total credit exposures x risk weighting).

- Market risk capital requirement (that is, 12.5 times capital charge for market risk).

- Operational risk capital requirement (that is, 12.5 times capital charge for operational risk).

4.3.2   The Pillars of Basel II

This section discusses the structure of Basel II and the features of the Pillars.

Pillar 1

Credit Risk Measurement, three measurement methods are available:

1   The Standardized Approach (TSA)

TSA allows the use of external ratings from credit rating agencies for wholesale credits (there are other rules for Retail) in order to determine the probability of default (PD). There are fixed risk weights per asset class. And, there is some (limited) capital relief for credit risk mitigation (including collateral).

2   Foundation-Internal Rating Based Approach (F-IRBA).

The F-IRB method allows banks to use their own models for estimating the probability of default (PD). Supervisors will provide the estimates for loss given default (LGD) and exposure at default (EAD); as well as some maturity data. Also, there is some relief for credit risk mitigation.

3   Advanced-Internal Rating Based Approach (A-IRB)

The A-IRB method allows banks to use their internal models to calculate PDs, LGDs and EADs. And there is full capital relief available for credit risk mitigation.

Technical Elements:

PD (Probability of Default) means the probability of default within one year for an obligor.

LGD (Loss Given Default) is the estimate of loss as a percentage of the exposure at default (EAD). LGD must reflect economic losses, that is, the inflows and outflows of cash or assets discounted at an appropriate rate.

EAD (Exposure at Default) is the total expected exposure of the bank in a facility at the time of obligor default.

The primary methodological difference between the TSA and the two Internal Ratings Based Approaches is that the Standardized Approach allows the use of external ratings from credit rating agencies and the Internal Ratings Based approaches allows the use of the bank's own internal rating system's loss estimates.

The primary methodological difference between F-IRB and A-IRB approaches is that the F-IRBA method allows banks to use their own estimates of PD, although supervisors provide the estimates for LGD and EAD while in the A-IRBA banks are allowed to use their internal processes to calculate PDs, LGDs and EADs.

Market Risk Measurement, two measurement methods are available:

1   The Standardized Approach (TSA).

TSA uses a building-blocks approach. The capital charge for each risk category is determined separately. Within the interest rate and equity position risk categories, separate capital charges for specific risk and the general market risk arising from debt and equity positions are calculated. For commodities and foreign exchange, there is only a general market risk capital requirement.

2   Internal Model Approach (IMA).

Unless an institution's exposure to a particular risk factor, such as commodity prices, is insignificant, the internal measurement system requires institutions to have an integrated risk measurement system that captures the broad risk factor categories (that is, interest rates, exchange rates, equity prices and commodity prices). Thus, institutions that start to use models for one or more risk factor categories will, over time, be expected to extend the models to all their market risks. Mixing of approaches is not permissible.

Operational Risk Measurement, three measurement methods are available:

1 Basic Indicator Approach (BIA).

   The BIA sets the capital requirement for operational risk at a fixed percentage of the bank's total average annual gross income.

2 The Standard Approach (TSA).

   In the TSA activities are divided into eight business lines. A capital charge is required for each one of these business lines. This capital charge is a fixed percentage of the average annual gross income of each business line.

3 Advanced Measurement Approach (AMA).

   Banks the world over have been developing different methodologies for the measurement of an operational risk capital charge under AMA. The Basel Committee has been less prescriptive in respect of the AMA, which is based on an estimate of operational risk derived from a bank's internal risk measurement system and are, therefore, expected to be more risk sensitive than the other two approaches.

Pillar 2

This section discusses embedding Basel II and the application of the Use Test

A key requirement of Pillar 2 is the implementation of a bank-wide programme of robust risk management processes and techniques (or Internal Capital Adequacy Assessment Process PILLAR 2/ICAAP).

Pillar 2 requires that integrated risk management systems be embedded into the bank's operations and management.

Thus, an important requirement of Pillar 2 is to embed risk management processes into the lines of business so that it becomes business as usual or normal business operations.

The focus is on embedding the philosophies, concepts and tools of Basel II into the Bank's internal processes, activities, people and systems. Therefore, the requirement is to embed; not just an "add on" using a bureaucratic approach.

Embedding is, in fact, a dynamic process. This includes:

o   Incorporating the concept of risk into the DNA of the bank.

o   Risk management incorporated into the fabric of the line businesses.

The Use Test must be passed.

The Use Test refers to an organisational way of life that acknowledges risks and addresses them effectively. The Use Test demonstrates that risk management processes are truly integrated into the management of the business and support functions throughout the organization.

The Use Test focuses on using risk-based models for commercial use, wherever possible.

Risk management should be viewed not as a separate process or activity, but as a competency that is embedded in the organization.

This competence enhances the organization's ability to manage uncertainty and volatility.

Therefore, the PILLAR 2/ICAAP should form an integral part of the management (not just risk management) process and decision-making culture of the bank.

Benefits of Pillar 2

• Capital Efficiency. This will educe the minimum capital requirement and hence cost of capital and more efficient use of current capital via greater scope for business expansion.

- Improved Risk Management Practices resulting in:
  - More focused risk-taking
  - Reduced losses through inappropriate activity
  - Increased capacity for risk-adjusted pricing
  - Cost efficiency through appliance of risk-based control environment
- Reduction in regulatory supervision so the regulator will have greater confidence in advanced risk management framework.

Pillar 3

This section describes the background, purpose and importance of Pillar 3.

Background of Pillar 3

Pillar 3 is intended to complement Pillars 1 and 2, consistent with the way the bank assesses and manages risks and proportionate to its degree of sophistication.

The purpose of Pillar 3 is to complement the minimum capital requirements of credit, market and operational risks in Pillar 1 and the supervisory review process to assess a firm's risks, risk management practices and the capital requirements of the firm addressed in Pillar 2.

Pillar 3 is particularly important with respect to the Basel II Accord because of its reliance in Basel II on internal methodologies that allow banks greater discretion in determining their capital needs.

Pillar 3 encourages market discipline through risk transparency. Basel II aims to encourage market discipline by allowing market participants to assess a bank's capital adequacy from disclosure of its capital, risk exposures and risk assessment processes.

Purpose of Pillar 3

> The purpose of Pillar 3 is to complement the minimum capital requirements of Pillar 1 and the supervisory review process addressed in Pillar 2.
>
> Pillar 3 aims to encourage market discipline by allowing stakeholders to assess a bank's capital adequacy from disclosure of its capital, risk exposures and risk assessment processes.
>
> Basel II seeks to encourage market discipline by developing a set of disclosure requirements that allow market participants to assess key information about a bank's risk profile and level of capitalisation.

Why is Pillar 3 so important?

> Pillar 3 is particularly important because of the reliance in Basel II on internal methodologies that allow banks greater discretion in determining their capital needs.
>
> Key points on Pillar 3's disclosure and transparency are as follows:
>
> o   Investors demand transparency to maintain trust in management.
>
> o   Solid corporate governance reflected in clear comprehensive disclosure.
>
> o   A somewhat flexible concept was devised in order to achieve market discipline.
>
> o   Forced disclosure of loss rates (credit risk and operational risk) impacts a bank's credit ratings.
>
> o   Risk and capital will be increasingly used by the market as information becomes familiar.
>
> o   Regulatory approval will be a strong sign of market acceptance of information.

4.3.3   The Basel II approach

Unlike Basel I, which represented more of a one-size-fits-all approach to risk management, Basel II offers banks an opportunity to create an approach to risk measurement that is more consistent with their own risk management frameworks.

For example, in the AMA for risk, banks can use their own internal models, subject to supervisory approval, to determine the capital to be held for operational risk. Banks are expected to use four key elements in developing these models: internal loss data, external loss data, scenario analysis and qualitative factors reflecting the business environment and internal control systems. Thus Basel II makes risk management more quantitative. In addition, the process of developing and maintaining loss databases is a huge undertaking which will require companies to define operating processes, dissect the organization and capture information in a way that is most meaningful to the organization.[14]

Basle or Basel, which one is correct?

The Bank of International Settlements is based in a bilingual Swiss city for which there were two spellings of its name, which has caused some confusion in referring to their documents. In 2001, the city voted on whether it would take for its official spelling "Basel", a German word or "Basle", the French spelling. The citizens voted in favour of the German "Basel" and the Bank of International Settlements has followed suit and spells it Basel as well.

4.4   International regulations

Solvency II is a fundamental review of the capital adequacy regime for European insurers and reinsurers, planned to take effect from October 2012. It aims to establish a revised set of EU-wide capital requirements, valuation techniques and risk management standards that will replace the current Solvency I requirements.[15]

14 Web Page - August 4, 2003, "Basel II yields increased focus on managing operational risks" By Dixie Walters KnowledgeLeader contributing writer, KnowledgeLeader by Protiviti Inc.
15 Discussion paper 08 / 4 (September, 2008) - Financial Services Authority - Insurance Risk Management: The Path To Solvency II, Financial Services Authority, London, UK

A key objective of Solvency II is to ensure that insurance firms are well managed and have adequate financial resources.[16]

4.4.1   Solvency II, requirements

Solvency II introduces economic risk-based solvency requirements. It differs from Solvency I in that it is more risk sensitive, and more entity specific, moving away from one size fits all approach. The Total Balance Sheet approach puts new focus on assets not found in Solvency I which is more liability based. In addition to insurance risks (life and general insurance), insurers will need to hold capital against market risk, credit risk and operational risk. However, it is clear from Solvency II that capital is not the only way to mitigate against failures. Solvency II will for the first time compel insurers specifically to focus on and devote significant resources to the identification, measurement and proactive management of risks.

While current Solvency focus is backward or historical looking, Solvency II will be more forward looking requiring, for example, scenario analysis. Further, there will be a new Own Risk and Solvency Assessment (ORSA) requirement. Solvency II's emphasis on a need to identify risks of an undertaking will assist supervisors in understanding specific firm risks.

Solvency II, quantitative requirements

Minimum Capital Requirement:
  (MCR) new, if this is breached, insurer may not write new business.

Solvency Capital Requirement (SCR):
  new, first warning if SCR level is breached.

* SCR based on Value at Risk (VaR): measure at 99.5% over 1 year horizon – all risks included (insurance, market, credit, operational).

---

16 ibid.

- SCR can be calculated with European Standard Formula or an approved internal model, for example AMA-type.

4.4.2   E-Solvency II, Three Pillar Approach

Pillar 1

Quantitative Requirements[17]

In the detailed design of the approach, Solvency II has looked at the range of risks that were considered within Basel and chosen to include all quantifiable risks within Pillar 1. This includes insurance risk (arising out of the volatility within the underwriting and reserves) and is intended to reflect the variety of risks and exposures that different insurers face in aggregate.

Pillar 2

Requirements for the governance and risk management of insurers.
Also capital add-on.

Pillar 3

Supervisory reporting and transparency requirements.

4.4.3   Introduction and application

Solvency II applies to all EU insurers and reinsurers with gross premium income exceeding EUR 5m or gross technical provisions in excess of EUR 25m.[18]

---

17 *Banking – Basel Briefing 11", September 2006, Financial Services, KPMG International*

18 *Discussion paper 08 / 4 (September, 2008) - Financial Services Authority - Insurance Risk Management: The Path To Solvency II, Financial Services Authority, London, UK.*

4.4.4   Comparing Solvency II and Basel II

Similarities

Both Basel II and Solvency II have similar aims, which are:

- To create a prudential framework more appropriate to the true risks facing the respective organisations (credit institutions for Basel II and insurance companies for Solvency II).

- To create incentives for companies to understand and manage their own risks better.

Both Basel II and Solvency II:

- Use the Three Pillar approach.

- Move away from one size fits all capital approach (for example flat % for capital allocation). But they use different methods of calculating capital (such as TSA and AMA)

- Increase focus on operational risk calculation versus prior regulatory regimes.

Differences

- Basel II is international, while Solvency II is specific to the European Union.

- Insurers have market, credit, liquidity (considered small by some) and operational risk like banks but also have actuarial risk and other insurer specific risks (risk is the business of insurers). There are three keys risks in Solvency II that are unique for insurers. First, underwriting risk, which is the risk that claims are higher than expected; this can be caused by external or internal factors. The second is actuarial risk, which is the risk that actuarial assumptions are wrong (mainly life related or longer term policies). Finally there is claims risk, which is the risk that claims are mismanaged.

- Insurers in UK already have Individual Capital Assessment process, thus less radical change from Solvency I to Solvency II than for Basel I to Basel II

- Economic approach to assets and liabilities.

  Solvency II aims for a framework that is based more on an economic and market-consistent approach, reflecting the realistic values of assets and liabilities and considering the way they interact.[19]

- Diversification Benefits

  A significant difference is the aim of Solvency II to include recognition of diversification benefits more transparently and in a manner unique to each organisation. Basel II addresses diversification by assuming a general level of diversification and incorporating this into the general calibration. In addition, some company specific diversification is allowed within operational risk and market risk. However the total capital requirement is obtained simply by adding up the capital required for each individual risk. Those groups lacking diversification are expected to add to the capital requirement in Pillar.

  Diversification, though, is at the core of insurance business and can vary hugely across organisations depending on the nature and variety of classes of business written and the risk management strategies followed.

  o Solvency II aims to find a way to incorporate diversification (and concentration risk).

  o Company-wide diversification benefits are also recognised by Solvency II and the distribution of diversification benefits from the head office down to subsidiaries.

---

19 *"Banking – Basel Briefing 11", September 2006, Financial Services, KPMG International*

- Use of Full Internal Models – this is the biggest difference.[20]

4.4.5   Use and approval of full internal models

The most significant difference between Basel II and Solvency II is the treatment of full internal models. Pillar 1 of Basel II only allows a full internal portfolio model approach for market risk and operational risk. For credit risk, which tends to be the largest component of a bank's capital requirement, companies are only allowed to use internal models to determine the parameters (probability of default, loss given default and exposure at default) to feed into a supervisory prescribed model. In the field of operational risk for Basel II, firms can choose the AMA backed up by a sophisticated internal model (including scenario and loss distribution approaches).

Solvency II aims to allow a full internal model approach. This reflects the broad range and scale of risks faced by different insurers and allows them the opportunity to build models that better reflect the interaction between risks in their own firms and also the mitigation resulting from the risk management techniques used (including diversification).[21]

Solvency II permits firms to apply for approval to use full or partial internal models for the calculation of their regulatory capital requirements, as an alternative to applying the results of the standard formula. The internal modelling activity is required to be integrated into the risk management activity of the firm. To meet Solvency II requirements, firms will need to continue to develop their modelling and to integrate their risk and capital management frameworks.

For firms intending to seek approval for their internal model, they will require approval to use an internal model by demonstrating compliance with several mandated tests and requirements, including use,

---

20 *ibid.*
21 *ibid.*

statistical quality, data, documentation, calibration and profit and loss attribution. In addition, activities such as sensitivity, stress and scenario testing will also need to be evidenced.[22]

4.4.6 Pillar 1: Demonstrating adequate financial resources

Under Solvency II, the SCR may be calculated either by using a standard formula or through an approved internal model. All firms will need to be familiar with the standard formula for calculating the SCR.[23]

Solvency II provides for two different solvency requirements: The and The MCR. The SCR represents the required capital for regulatory solvency, and is calibrated to give protection against a 1 in 200 chance loss event that basic own funds will remain positive (99.5% value-at-risk over a one year period). The MCR represents the level below which capital resources must not fall in order not to lose the regulatory authorisation to write new business. It is calibrated to give protection against a 1 in 7 chance loss event that basic own funds will remain positive (85% value-at-risk over a one year period).

The SCR may be calculated either by using a standard formula or an approved internal model. The MCR (for non-life companies) is calculated using a simple calculation based on technical provisions and amount of annual premiums. However, in order to maintain a link between the MCR and SCR, the MCR is restricted to a corridor of 25%-45% of the SCR. This link is necessary since supervisory intervention needs to be scaled-up as the financial position of the insurer (of which the MCR and SCR are representations) deteriorates.

The Pillar 1 elements of Solvency II sets out the quantitative requirements: market consistent valuation of assets and liabilities as well as risk sensitive SCR and

---

22 Discussion paper 08 / 4 (September, 2008) - Financial Services Authority - Insurance Risk Management: The Path To Solvency II, Financial Services Authority, London, UK
23 ibid.

MCR calculations. In addition to this, insurers need to demonstrate they have sufficient financial resources which are of the right quality to meet the SCR and MCR. These resources are known as the "own funds" or "excess of assets over liabilities" on the Solvency II balance sheet. Own funds are further split into: (a) basic own funds (that is, on-balance sheet) and; (b) ancillary own funds (that is, off-balance sheet). The quality of these own funds is determined by considering their paid-up status, loss absorbency (in a going concern or in a wind-up), subordination, permanence or sufficient duration, ability to be locked-in on breach of the SCR, flexibility of coupon or dividend payments and existence of the incentive to redeem.

Depending on the quality assessment, the own funds are classified into the three tiers in order of reducing quality: tier 1 (basic own funds only), tier 2 (basic and ancillary own funds) and tier 3 (basic and ancillary own funds). Furthermore, there are rules governing how much of each tier can be used to cover the SCR; the MCR must strictly be covered by basic own finds from tier 1 and tier 2 only.

4.4.7 Internal Model

A firm's internal model (IM) should be integrated within its overall risk management and decision-making activities. Most importantly, an internal model should be used to quantify risks and assess a firm's economic capital. The Solvency II directive does not define specifically the internal model required to be used but it is described as follows:

> '... internal model refers to "a risk management system developed by an insurer to analyse the overall risk position, to quantify risks and to determine the economic capital required to meet those risks. An internal model may also be used to determine the insurer's regulatory capital requirements on the basis of the insurer's specific

risk profile and the defined level of safety of the solvency regime."[24]

In Solvency II, an IM can be used to determine the SCR. The Directive allows this in recognition of the broad range and scale of risks faced by different insurers as well as to better reflect the interaction between risks in the various firms and also the differing mitigations resulting from the various risk management techniques used.

Solvency II permits firms to apply for approval to use their full or partial internal models (where parts of the SCR calculation make use of the standardised formula) for the calculation of their regulatory SCR capital requirements, as an alternative to applying the results of the standard formula. The internal modelling activity is required to be integrated into the risk management activity of the firm (that is, the need to integrate risk and capital management frameworks). Approval to use an internal model will require the firm to demonstrate compliance with several mandated tests and requirements, including use, statistical quality, data, documentation, calibration and profit and loss attribution. Activities such as sensitivity, stress and scenario testing will also need to be evidenced. In addition, the firm will need to demonstrate that it meets the requirements of the use test, such that the IM is widely employed in and plays an important role in the managing of the business. Demonstrating compliance with this test is a key prerequisite for model approval.

4.4.8 The Use Test

The Use Test requires the insurer to demonstrate that there is sufficient discipline in its internal model development and application such that it is 'widely used in and plays an important role in' the management of the firm. Through this, supervisors can be sure that an internal model is appropriate to the business, if it is

---

24. *Financial Service Authority - DP 08/4 – Insurance Risk Management: The Path to Solvency II, September, 2008, Paragraph 5.6.*

widely used and plays an important role in how the firm measures and manages risk in its business.[25]

4.4.9   Pillar 2: Systems of governance

Under Pillar 2, the company is required to develop and embed a formal set of governance requirements. These include an effective risk management system which is owned and implemented by the company's senior management risk management system such as that it is able to identify, measure, monitor and report on all risks which the company faces. Specifically, the company must consider all risks to which it is, or could be, exposed to, with the risk management system fully integrated as a fundamental part of the running of the firm. Furthermore, the risk management system is required to play a key role in calculating and managing regulatory capital. This means that the company must consider all risks that are included in the calculation of the SCR as well as the risks that are not, or not fully, captured in the calculation. To fulfil this requirement the company must first be able to monitor and understand all the risks to which it is exposed, by having a robust risk management system in place. Solvency II necessitates the full integration of risk and capital management activities, so that any internal model is embedded within the business, consistent with the Use Test.

Another governance requirement is the implementation of a formalised, Pillar 2, risk-based evaluation of the whole firm. This evaluation should be based on Management's chosen business model, business plan, risk appetite, the appropriateness of technical provisions and investments, the ability to meet policyholder obligations, the level of capital required to run the company and the appropriateness of the capital requirements calculation. The results of this ORSA are reported to the company's supervisor and, as applicable, through the annual Solvency and Financial

---

25 Solvency II, Directive 2009/138/EC, of the European Parliament and of the Council, 25 November 2009, Article 120.

Condition report (SFCR). The ORSA will compare actual capital available against regulatory capital requirements and, where different, the firm's chosen level of economic capital. It will also compare key assumptions against evidence of their correctness and consider future capital requirements or management actions. The ORSA can be defined as the entirety of the processes and procedures employed to identify, assess, monitor, manage and report the short and long term risks the company faces or may face and to determine the own funds necessary to ensure that the overall (not just regulatory) solvency needs are met at all times. A robust risk management function supports the Company to undertake a robust ORSA, which links together the firm's own view of the risks it has within its business and its own solvency needs. Therefore, the ORSA is an internal risk assessment process whose objective is to ensure that senior management has conducted its own review of the risks which the company is exposed to, and that it holds sufficient capital against those exposures.

4.4.10   Pillar 3: Reporting requirements

Under the External Reporting and Disclosure requirements of Pillar 3, the company is required to produce significant quantitative and qualitative information on a regular basis. This information will be disclosed to the public as part of the SFCR, and also in private reporting to the regulator, as part of the Report to Supervisor (RTS). Much of the underlying information and analysis for the SFCR and RTS will be drawn from the company's own risk and solvency assessment and its financial statements.

The SFCR is produced on an annual basis and includes the annual Quantitative Reporting Templates (QRTs). As part of its SFCR, the company will be required to disclose its regulatory capital requirements, including any material breaches of its MCR and SCR, even if subsequently resolved, as well as the details of any capital add-ons if applicable. In addition to key financial information, such as the SII Balance Sheet and Income

Statements, the company will provide a description of its business and financial performance, its systems of governance and the different risks it faces, including for each risk category the risk exposure, concentration, mitigation and sensitivity. Quarterly QRTs will also be required to be publicly disclosed by the company.

The RTS includes all information necessary for the purposes of supervision and as with the SFCR covers both qualitative and quantitative reporting. The RTS is required in full once every 5 years with a nil return or material changes reported annually.[26]

4.4.11   Solvency II

Solvency II will bring the creation of a new Solvency regime for insurers across the European Union and Israel, and will update Solvency I. The establishment is driven by the desire of the EU to facilitate development of a single market in insurance, and ensure adequate consumer protection. This will lead to more harmonised rules across the EU, replacing the current patchwork of country specific insurance legislation.

See *Comparing Solvency II and Basel II, page 85.*

It should be noted that other political jurisdictions outside the EU are implementing regulations similar to Solvency II for their insurance companies.

4.4.12   Basel III

As a result of the difficulties experienced by many banks, because they did not manage their liquidity and overall operations in a prudent manner during the financial crisis that began in 2007, the Basel Committee has established reforms to strengthen global capital and liquidity regulations. The Committee's goals are to promote a more resilient banking sector, and to have greater international harmonization of liquidity risk supervision, reporting and monitoring.

---

26 *Discussion paper 08 / 4 (September, 2008) - Financial Services Authority - Insurance Risk Management: - The Path To Solvency II, Financial Services Authority, London, UK.*

Basel III is an international agreement designed to improve stability in the banking industry in the aftermath of the 2007-09 financial crisis by addressing shortcomings in capital requirements and other matters, such as liquidity, particularly for larger, internationally active banking organizations.

The determination of capital is an important one for banks as the result of additional capital requirements means increased costs as well as limiting banks' ability for further growth. When banks are required to hold more capital, then there is either less money available for giving out loans or higher interest rates need to be charged to borrowers.

The Basel III capital rules bring significant changes to the financial system by ensuring the maintenance of strong capital positions and other related enhancements.

In the United States, the Basel III capital reforms are in addition to other changes required by the Dodd-Frank Wall Street Reform and Consumer Protection Act (which covers derivatives, proprietary trading – the Volcker Rule – and consumer lending). Together, these requirements are in many ways tougher than those in most other jurisdictions worldwide as the combined impact of all these American regulatory changes is very significant.

Under the third international Basel framework, the rules includes a new minimum ratio of common equity tier 1 capital to risk-weighted assets of 4.5% and a common equity tier 1 capital conservation buffer of 2.5% of risk-weighted assets that will apply to all supervised financial institutions. The rule also raises the minimum ratio of tier 1 capital to risk-weighted assets from 4% to 6%. On the quality of capital side, the final rule emphasizes common equity tier 1 capital, the most loss-absorbing form of capital, and implements strict eligibility criteria for regulatory capital instruments.

The Accord also adopts a capital conservation buffer for all banking organizations, as well as another, known as a "countercyclical capital buffer," for advanced approaches banking organizations (ranging between 0 to 2.5%). The capital conservation buffer is intended to ensure that institutions are able to absorb losses in stress periods lasting for a number of years. One the other hand, the countercyclical capital buffer's goal is to achieve the broader macro-prudential goal of protecting the banking sector and the real economy from the system-wide risks stemming from the boom-bust evolution such that a buffer is required during periods of excessive credit growth and is released in an economic downturn.

To help prevent an excessive build-up of leverage on institutions' balance sheets, the final rule introduces a new non-risk based leverage ratio to supplement the risk-based capital framework. The leverage ratio's purpose is to counter the build-up of extreme on- and off-balance sheet leverage. Therefore, in addition to the risk-weighted capital rules, a minimum leverage ratio of 4% will apply to all banks.

These rules have various phase-in timelines.

It should be noted that Basel II gives banking organizations a choice between two methods for calculating risk-weighted assets for credit risk, which comprise the denominator of a banking organization's risk-based capital ratios. One is the standardized approach that permits them to measure credit risk using metrics and risk-weightings prescribed by regulation. Another is the advanced approach (or internal ratings-based approach) that allows banking organizations to use their internal models and ratings systems to measure credit risk, subject to regulatory approval.

To complement these principles and further strengthen its liquidity framework, the Committee developed two minimum standards for funding liquidity – the Liquidity Coverage Ratio (LCR) and the Net Stable Funding Ratio (NSFR) – which achieve two separate but complementary objectives, both of which are important.

4.5 Standards of governance

4.5.1 Defining risks

The firm faces a variety of risks. It is important to distinguish between:

- Risk of ruin – which refers to those risks that can have a potential impact on the firm's financial position.

- Risks to business objectives – which refers to risks that could potentially impact the firm's future strategy, possible loss of reputation and ultimately future profitability.

4.5.2 Why corporate governance matters

Fundamentally, corporate governance makes good commercial sense. Having well defined systems and controls, and clear reporting lines and accountability enables the production of good management information to produce sound decision-making. This in turn should demonstrate to analysts and share-holders the orderliness in organisation that produces confidence in the company in the market place. The Corporate Governance Framework essentially comprises three pillars: (1) the RM Policies, (2) the Risk-related Committees and (3) the Key Roles and Responsibilities.

4.5.3 Governance framework

Corporate Governance consists of three principal elements:

1 A pervasive culture and management approach which underpins the overall operation of the firm and ensures that its business is conducted in a fit and proper manner.

2 A company-wide governance framework which prescribes constraints in the form of rules, processes, organisation and responsibilities, and within which management operates.

3   The execution of that governance framework through the fulfilment and observance of its rules, processes and roles.

The governance framework should be comprised of a set of inter-linking company-wide policies, committee structures and key roles. A governance framework needs to be understood in the context of its many components and interactions.

First, the business objectives must be clear specified. There must be preset metrics for the measurement of the firm's traction in meeting these objectives. Next, business operations are established to meet these objectives. This includes setting up the required organizational structure, policies, procedures, controls and staffing. At this point, the governance framework is designed, constructed, implemented and embedded. Both internal stakeholders and regulators require assurance that the risk management (including risk standards and processes) and governance frameworks adequately captures all material risks. The governance framework establishes the rules, processes, organisation and responsibilities, within which management operates.

There are three lines of defence in the governance framework. Line management is the first, having primary responsibility for the owning of risk. The line management or business risk takers have ownership of risk and primary responsibility for the identification, management, monitoring and reporting of risks.

The risk function is the second line of defence which provides challenge and support for line management, the first line. The risk and governance functions (for example, compliance) provide support and challenge on the completeness, accuracy and consistency of risk assessments, and adequacy of mitigating action plans. They are also responsible for the risk management methodologies and frameworks to assist the first line and ensuring risks are reported appropriately.

The third line provides independent supervision and assurance. Internal audit provides assurance over the robustness of the risk management framework and appropriateness and effectiveness of the control environment.

Governance framework

Figure 17 shows how all of the first, second and third lines of defence use various methods, tools and models to assist them in executing their mandates. This includes the central system for risks and controls, which includes the identification, assessment, managing, reporting, monitoring and review of exposures and associated mechanisms for required control.

The people and culture (such as organization structure, resource allocation, employee competency, staffing tools, management supervision, employee irregularities and compliance to HR policies) is critical throughout.

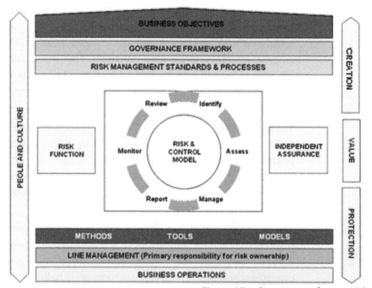

Figure 17 – Governance framework

A systematic and consistent approach is required to protect the business resources against losses and unexpected events so that objectives of the company can be achieved without unnecessary interruptions.

By all of the above being effectively executed, value is created and achieved.

4.5.4 Risk-related policies

Each risk-related policy should have a functional owner who maintains the currency of the policy, ensures it is appropriately communicated and oversees and monitors adherence to the policy at an appropriate level of materiality. Key functional areas with ownership for firm policies include risk, compliance, and financial control.

Business units should be responsible for local implementation of company-wide policies; thereby ensuring the business is run in a manner which conforms to these general policies and establishing as required more detailed or additional local policies in accordance with their local environment.

4.5.5 Risk-related committees

There should be well established risk-related committees in place. These committees exist to make decisions relating to certain transactions and oversee elements of the function. Key committees of this type include the derivatives, credit, treasury, life and general insurance risk committees.

4.5.6 Risk-related roles

The company should support the company's governance framework through a number of different risk-focused roles, some pure governance, some development, and some a mix of both. Ultimately, all senior managers have responsibilities that support the governance of the company. It is therefore vital that all senior manager role profiles accurately reflect the responsibilities of the role, and the key systems and controls on which the role relies. In addition to internally defined roles, the regulators require the company to identify individuals in specific roles that exert a significant influence over the affairs of our regulated firms.

Internal corporate governance summary

Figure 18 illustrates the structure of internal corporate governance. Corporate governance is commonly referred to as the system by which firms are directed and controlled. It is the process by which company objectives are established, achieved and monitored.

Figure 18 – Internal Corporate Governance

Corporate governance is concerned with the relationships and responsibilities between the board, management, shareholders and other relevant stakeholders within a legal and regulatory framework (and, sometimes, a best practices framework too).

Using the "three lines of defence" model, corporate governance consists of three principal elements:

- A pervasive culture and management approach which underpins the overall operation of the firm.

- A company-wide governance framework which prescribes constraints in the form of rules, processes, organisation and responsibilities, and within which management operates.

- The execution of that governance framework through the fulfilment and observance of its rules, processes and roles.

The governance framework ensures that specific matters or transactions follow a prescribed process. Decisions made on such matters or transactions are management decisions, except where they relate to the definition of the governance framework.

4.6 Sarbanes-Oxley

Sarbanes-Oxley (SOX) is an important component of the corporate governance program of most large financial institutions. Its reach extends far beyond the United States. For example, it applies to foreign subsidiaries of large American corporations. And many jurisdictions have issued legislation similar to SOX, for example in Europe it is known as Euro-SOX and in Japan it is J-SOX while in Canada it is C-SOX.

4.6.1 What is Sarbanes-Oxley?

In the United States, the Sarbanes-Oxley Act (July 2002) places heavy emphasis on good governance, risk identification and related controls. SOX requires management to perform an assessment of its internal controls over financial reporting and to provide a written report detailing the effectiveness of those internal controls, within the bank's annual report.

Section 302 outlines management's responsibilities for the content of all public filings with the SEC and includes disclosure controls and procedures expected of the CEO and CFO. It requires the CEO and CFO to certify that: internal controls have been designed and established to ensure material information is made known to them in a timely basis, the effectiveness of the internal controls has been assessed within the 90 days and all significant deficiencies in design or operation of the internal controls have been reported to the Audit Committee and the external auditors.

Section 404 outlines the specific expectations of management regarding financial controls. Management must establish and maintain an adequate internal control structure and procedures for financial reporting, report on the effectiveness of the internal controls, report significant deficiencies to the Audit Comm. and report material weaknesses to the public.

The Public Company Accounting Oversight Board (PCAOB) Auditing Standard No. 2, approved by the SEC June 17, 2004, provides guidance on the audit requirements established in SOX. The Standard requires management to assess itself against a recognized framework, such as the COSO framework.

4.6.2   Determining scope

The first step in determining scope is to review the general ledger and identify significant financial accounts. Having identified the significant accounts and the applicable lines of business, it is then necessary to understand the processes and sub-processes that contribute to those accounts (for example, how a loan gets recorded in the loan accounting system). A thorough understanding of a process should cover the five steps of the transaction life cycle: initiate, authorize, process, record and report.

4.6.3   Assessing the adequacy of controls and reporting of deficiencies

All key controls identified and documented should be assessed for their design adequacy. This does not require testing; it is only an assessment from a design perspective. If there are deficiencies identified from the analysis of design you need to classify them. There are three classifications of deficiency: material weakness (the big one), significant deficiency and internal control deficiency.

4.6.4   Evaluating effectiveness of controls and reporting of deficiencies

Operating effectiveness testing is about testing the control activities to ensure that they are operating consistently and effectively. Operating effectiveness of controls should be tested at a frequency determined in accordance with the risk ranking of the sub-processes or control. The testing objective is to identify and confirm that the control works. If there are deficiencies identified from testing they should be classified.

4.6.5 Controlling risk

With regard to SOX, financial reporting risks are the issues or circumstances that could cause misstatements in the financial statements. Financial reporting risks and controls are documented in a control matrix. The Control matrix is the tool for documenting information related to financial controls. The matrix serves to guide control activity and testing as well as to store key information about both.

A key control is an activity or procedure that by its effective design and operation would significantly increase the probability of preventing or detecting an error or misstatement in the financial reporting. Key controls are essential in order to achieve the Financial Statement assertions. Controls can be preventative (helps a risk from occurring in the first place) or detective. If a control is not key, it is then known as a supporting control.

When assessing risks and determining controls it is crucial to remember the assertions that management makes regarding the financial statements. The Financial Statement assertions indicate that management has control over all of the attributes and elements of the financial statements. The different types of assertions are: existence, occurrence (transactions actually occurred), completeness (all transactions recorded), and valuation (asset is correctly valued).

There are four types of tests used to verify the design and operating effectiveness of the controls:

- Inquiry (interview and ask)
- Examination (review documents)
- Observation
- Re-performance (tester may execute the control on a sample basis). Testing is sometimes called compliance testing (that is, making sure policy is being complied with).

Chapter 5,
Risk management and mitigation

Question 1

Luca Pacioli:

In operating a profit seeking enterprise (such as a trade guild), which is in fact done in our small city, what tools can be used to help minimise the risk to an acceptably low level?

We reply:

o   There are a number of ways to minimise risk. One way is to simply avoid the risk by adjusting the activities so that the risk no longer applies; the extreme case being to close down the area of exposure. Another way is to control the risk by establishing processes to monitor and/or manage a particular aspect of the risk.

Question 2

Luca Pacioli

To manage the profit seeking enterprise should we keep some money in the books of account as a safety cushion?

We reply:

o   Yes, we should. It is important to keep some funds segregated to ensure that in the event a risk occurs then there will be money available to meet this requirement and ensure the continued operation of the enterprise.

Question 3

Luca Pacioli:

How can the profit-seeking enterprise help ensure that all people involved in the endeavour be aware and consider risk?

We reply:

○ The key point is to try to fix or retain the idea of risk (and return) in the minds of all workers in the enterprise so that it becomes part of normal operations.

Question 4

Luca Pacioli:

How important is the concept of "risk culture"?

We reply:

○ To establish an effective risk management programme a key requirement is a pervasive culture and management approach which underpins the overall operation of the Group and ensures that its business is conducted in a fit and proper manner.

5.1 How to manage risk-risk management cycle

"The best we can do is size up the chances, calculate the risks involved, estimate our ability to deal with them, and then make our plans with confidence."

Henry Ford

"Take calculated risks. That is quite different from being rash."

General George S. Patton

At the heart of an Enterprise Risk Management system is the Internal Model. The IM is a representation of the risk and capital management processes which support management of the banking or insurance business. The IM assists management in articulating the overall risk profile of the business and in calculating the capital requirements of the current operations and plans as well as making decisions that take into account the risk and capital implications of those decisions.

The IM is a key part of the risk and capital assessment process, and model outputs influence a number of key business functions. The IM must have the right capabilities and granularity to meet the business needs (for users: decision-making on performance assessments and pricing). The scope of the IM must be wide enough to properly capture the business and risk profiles of the businesses of the applicable entities. Given the importance of the IMs to the running of the businesses, there will be constant internal pressure for model improvement and accuracy, which will also enhance the regulatory model-based capital calculation.

The model is driven by parameters supplied by the business functions; the business functions then use the consequent model outputs. The overall structure of the IM (in particular the outputs) is driven by the demands of the business users' requirements in a continual feedback loop. The ERM framework includes many elements such as risk management systems, risk policies, risk strategy and appetite, risk profile, risk register and governance.

The reporting/disclosures element is the processes and procedures employed to identify, assess, monitor, manage, and report the short and long term risks a firm faces or may face, and to determine the own funds necessary to ensure that overall capital needs are met at all times.

The use test demonstrates that the internal model is widely used and plays an important role in the firm's system of governance and in particular, its risk management system, decision-making processes and the reporting/disclosures system. Other tests, for example those which are specified by Solvency II, include statistical and data quality standards and validation standards.

Documentation is integral to the integrity of the IM and Internal Model Governance. A critical component is the standards for the required supporting documentation. The documentation standards include the following key requirements: clarity, completeness, accuracy, proportionality and an audit trail. The documentation will need to be sufficient and appropriate for a knowledgeable independent third party to understand it.

The IM is a key tool of risk management which quantifies the risk profile to determine the required economic and regulatory capital. The internal model covers all quantifiable material risks. The internal model is the collection of the required Inputs, capital calculation engine, generated outputs and related documentation. The calculation engine is the mathematical-based system which is used for the quantification of capital requirements for the risk categories specified.

Assumptions are of two types: (i) made throughout the IM where there is little or no internal or external data available for IM input and key assumptions are made using expert judgment and (ii) other required assumptions as applicable. External models are defined as the use of third party models to feed the capital calculation engine.

The internal model governance processes ensure the adequacy and effectiveness of the IM. Internal model governance ensures that the information from the model is delivered on time, complete and accurate, and also acts as a point of request for ad-hoc uses.

Design of an Enterprise Risk Management system and cycle

The Risk Management Framework (see Figure 19) is central in understanding the business model and how the business operates by way of the annual business processes and day-to-day businesses processes. The annual business process includes strategic planning and target setting, where senior management takes commitments from the business and models the financial impacts of these commitments. This includes calculating the capital requirements of the current operations and plans as the Internal Capital Model (equivalent to the Capital Calculation model) is used for the quantification of capital requirements for all risk categories. The day to day processes include: capital allocation and the link to pricing (how capital allocation and planning will influence the price of certain products), ALM and hedging.

Throughout, communications are important for the execution of the operation of the Risk Management Framework.

Economic capital is the unexpected loss protection utilised to ensure that the company will be able to operate independently as a going concern during periods of near catastrophic "worst case" loss scenarios.

Risk monitoring and reporting on business performance is important. Output from the Internal Capital Model provides outputs and analytics for the use of risk-adjusted performance measures to report and evaluate performance on the firm's activities. As well, Internal Risk Monitoring (through MI) includes monitoring and reporting on sources of risk to their respective management teams as well as senior management. The Internal Capital Model performs capital allocation by profit centres to produce risk metrics used to help assess risk-adjusted performance (for example, ROCA reporting).

Regarding corporate governance, the Internal Capital Model's outputs are used to assess and analyse for key decision-making in order to influence and shape business decisions, opportunities and planning (within the applicable risk appetite).

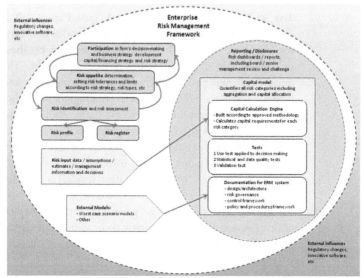

Figure 19 – ERM system and cycle

Risk Management Framework

Figure 20 describes the risk management framework. Establishing uses and embedding the Internal Capital Model are critical to this process. There is a need to demonstrate that the Internal Capital Model is widely used in its system of governance and in particular, in its risk management system, business decision-making processes and the internal and external reporting. The use test requires the company to demonstrate that there is sufficient discipline in its Internal Capital Model development and application such that it is widely used and plays an important role in the management of the firm. Through this, regulators can be sure that the Internal Capital Model is appropriate to the business. Demonstrating compliance with this test as an essential condition of Internal Capital Model approval. The use test supports the assertion that the Internal Capital Model is established and retained (that is, embedded) as part of firm's normal operation and into its everyday use.

Figure 20 – Risk management framework

5.2 Internal risk management

5.2.1 What does risk management do?

The primary duty of risk management is to determine the amount of capital which ensures the firm has sufficient capital resources available to meet its regulatory capital requirements and economic capital needs. To do this assessment, risk managers must understand what the business does; that is, its business model and its markets, products, processes and systems. The risk appetite or tolerance is the level of risk that a firm will accept for an individual risk or in total. The risk appetite can be seen as a series of boundaries authorised by management within which business units must operate.

Risk managers have these functions:

- Helping management to recognize, understand, measure and manage their risks.

- Understanding the need to promote growth and value creation as much as the need to control the downside of risk

- Recognizing that maximizing the risk/return relationship is the route to delivering improved shareholder value.

5.2.2 World Class risk management standards and programme

The implementation of a world class risk management function requires significant design and development of a number of fundamental building blocks using a detailed risk management architecture and design. First, a strong comprehensive corporate governance framework provides a solid foundation. Next, there must be a specific agreed risk vision for risk management, including identifying its roles, responsibilities, accountabilities and reporting lines. Subsequently, the risk policy framework (including risk management methodology) is developed and includes the risk governance framework and risk policies suite. A single, reliable and well-defined risk-related data-set is needed; this includes, for example, internal loss data for example, credit losses), loss scenarios (for operational risk purposes) and exposure information for example, the nature and size of the trading book for market risk purposes). Standard, transparent models for risk calculations (for each risk type) and economic capital allocations are needed. This provides the regulatory capital and economic capital systems required. To establish and maintain all of the above, mature project management practices, continuous process improvement and robust benefits business cases are required. Therefore high quality, motivated risk professionals are essential to achieve this programme.

Risk management building blocks

Figure 21 shows how world class risk management is established through the building blocks shown below. The foundation of the architecture of risk management is a comprehensive corporate governance framework, upon which risk policy framework is developed. Well-defined risk data for the purposes of operational, market, insurance and credit risk contribute to economic capital management. Fundamental building blocks including, but not limited to, the risk professionals themselves, are also essential to the building of this programme.

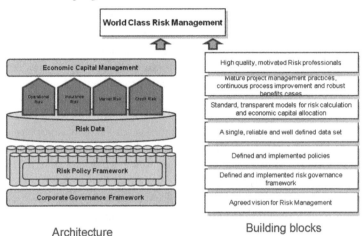

Architecture | Building blocks

Figure 21 – High Level risk management building blocks

5.2.3   Embedding risk management

The dictionary definition of "embed" is "to fix or retain a thought or idea in the mind." In the case of risk management, the focus is on embedding the philosophies, concepts and tools of Basel II, Solvency II and best practices into the firm's internal processes, activities, people and systems. Embedding is the process for establishing the operation of internal control frameworks, as defined by the 2nd line of defence, for example risk services, within the 1st line of defence, that is business areas, as part of their normal operation.

ERM is an embedded framework designed to be practical, and theoretically consistent, whose main components are fully integrated into the day to day management of risk. There are three main components:

- Governance.
- Organisation.
- Tools and modelling.

The ERM includes the governance structure of the company, the controls in place and the embeddedness of risk management.

Clear articulations of both risk strategy and risk appetite are key components in embedding risk management concepts across the organization. The fundamental idea is to embed risk management processes and people more deeply into the lines of business so that it becomes business as usual, or normal business operations. Therefore, the requirement is to embed; not just an add on using a bureaucratic approach. Embedding is, in fact, a dynamic process. Risk management should be viewed not as a separate process or activity, but as a competency that is embedded in the organization (thus, we think of it as things that need to be done). This competence enhances the organization's ability to manage uncertainty and volatility.

Some of the key areas of embedding requiring focus include:

- Ownership and Accountability.
- Risk Awareness.
- Governance.
- Enabling Risk Management processes.
- Aligning Risk Strategy/Appetite with Business Objectives and Strategy.
- Resourcing risk management adequately in the business.
- User friendliness of risk management.
- Value added of risk management to the business.

The principles of Basel II, Solvency II and best practices need to be deeply embedded into:

- High-level strategy.
- Management.
- Day-to-day business decisions.

Risk is a significant aspect of business activity in a market economy. Since risk-taking or transformation of risks constitutes a major characteristic of the banking business, it is especially important for banks to address risk management issues. The necessity from a business perspective has arisen from developments in the financial markets and the increasing complexity of the financial institutions business. These circumstances call for functioning systems which support the limitation and control of a firm's risk situation. This is achieved through a number of mechanisms including effective communications and a supportive environment provided by executive and senior management. The result is the inculcation of a risk culture throughout the organization, with concurrent risk-related roles and responsibilities identified and accepted.

There is a need to win the hearts and minds of non-risk management personnel in order to effectively embed key risk concepts throughout the organization. This can be done by various mechanisms: extending business unit accountabilities (for example, performance scorecards) to encompass risk management issues; such as incorporating the key concepts into job descriptions, performance evaluations and salary decisions. A risk-based approach should be used to establish a sound system of internal controls, and this system should be incorporated within the company's normal management and governance processes, not treated as a separate exercise to meet regulatory requirements. Furthermore, these risks must be genuinely owned by these groups. For example, responsibilities for the ownership of risks and controls should be included in all managers' position descriptions.

Whenever possible, there should be formalized incorporation of risks into all strategic and major tactical formulations. This can be achieved by establishing a connection between risk, capital requirements and returns on investments. Using the results of the risks models and systems, the risk management strategy is influenced by prioritising risk management activities.

Embedding risk management

One of the goals of risk management is to embed the philosophies, concepts and tools of Basel II, Solvency II and best practices into the firm's culture, thus making risk management a priority within the firm. This dynamic process is achieved through the ERM framework and its three key components of (i) governance, (ii) organization, (iii) tools and modelling. A model for embedding this ERM culture is shown in Figure 22.

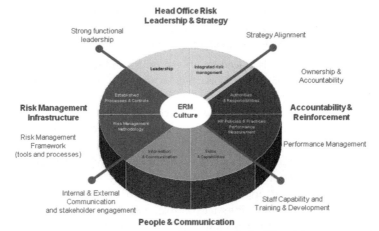

Figure 22 – Embedding risk management

5.2.4   Implementing and embedding risk

There is a need to develop and embed a risk culture across the entire firm. This includes all strategic business units and operating departments and applies whether the relevant activity is carried out in-house or outsourced.

Risk culture is the combined set of individual and corporate values, attitudes, competencies and behaviours that determines a firm's commitment and style of risk management. The result is improved risk awareness in the overall corporate culture, climate and mindset of the businesses and other groups (both profit and cost centres). A firm's culture of risk should include an interest in embedding incentives in order to increase compliance. For example, firms could consider possible reductions in capital charges where risks are reduced based on the actions of management (for example, improving internal controls).

Risk management should be incorporated into the fabric of line businesses. For example, this could be achieved by embedding processes to establish a continuous development process, which transforms from simple methods into a more complex system with enhanced control function. This would help incorporate risk management into the firm seamlessly, so that it becomes business as usual.

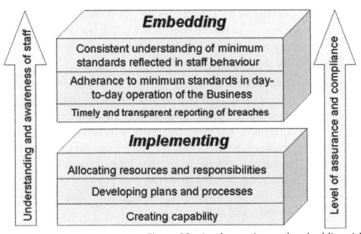

Figure 23 – Implementing and embedding risk

Implementing and embedding risk

Implementing risk into the firm includes creating capability to make this happen. Figure 23 shows how this includes developing the required plans and processes and allocating resources and responsibilities. Subsequent to the implementation of risk into the firm, is the embedding of risk. This includes timely and transparent reporting of breaches, adherence to minimum standards in day-to-day operation of the business as well as consistent understanding of minimum standards reflected in staff behaviour.

5.2.5 Management and success

Risk can be seen as an opportunity, which can prompt productive discussions on risks and opportunities; in fact, opportunity risk is a type of risk arising from the (usually deliberate) pursuit of business opportunities, with the potential to enhance (though it may inhibit) the achievement of business objectives.

Risk arises as much from the possibility that opportunities will not be realised as from the possibility that threats will happen. Therefore, risk refers to the uncertainty that surrounds future events and outcomes which have potential to expose the firm to losses, or to restrict or to threaten its ability to meet its objectives. Thus, risks can be considered as threats or perils. These definitions provide frameworks to analyse risks and inform appropriate action.

Understanding risks better will encourage sensible risk-taking and result in decision-making that takes into account the risk and capital implications of those decisions. For example, there will be occasions where the business can avoid the risk by choosing not to take a particular course of action. Thus, risk taking means accepting ownership of risk and primary responsibility for the identification, management, monitoring and reporting of risks.

Risk managers provide value to the business

Figure 24 shows how risk can be seen as (i) an opportunity, (ii) a threat, (iii) or an uncertainty. Risk managers must understand and incorporate all three of these perspectives in their decision-making in order to be successful.

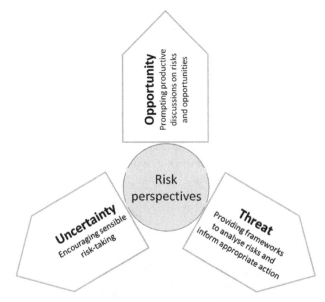

Figure 24 –Risk opportunities and threats

5.3   Risk and Capital

There is a strong and negatively correlated relationship between Risk and Capital. The capital assessment process reviews the firm's entire risk profile as a prerequisite to determining capital requirements. Therefore, capital assessments are important in risk management. There are three key capital-related steps in the risk management process: (i) assessment of the firm's risks, (ii) review of how the firm addresses those risks, (iii) calculation of how much current and future capital is necessary to cover those risks. This last point incorporates the concepts of capital planning and capital adequacy in Capital Management. Thus it is clear that risk and capital are connected and the latter must be considered in managing the former.

5.3.1   The risk and capital framework

The risk and capital framework should be incorporated into the business processes. The risk and capital framework should provide details for capital structure,

119

allocation and reporting, as well as assisting with the investment strategy and supporting management in decision making.

The framework also should assist with product design and pricing strategy (for example, helping to determine a full costing price strategy which includes acceptable return) and with performance measurement and executive compensation (for example, Risk Adjusted Rate of Return, RAROC). In addition, the risk and capital framework will assist with external communication.

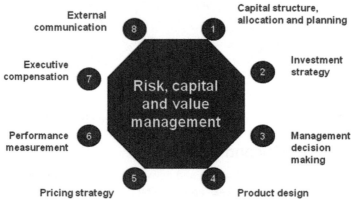

Figure 25 – Framework incorporated in business processes

The risk and capital framework

Figure 25 shows how the risk and capital framework should be incorporated into the eight business processes, to manage capital assessments.

Information received by management

Information received by management through reporting coupled with the output of financial quantification tools should inform risk-taking and decision-making through the planning and change element of the risk management cycle.

Figure 26 shows how this output information should be integral to the capital allocation, objective setting and business planning process.

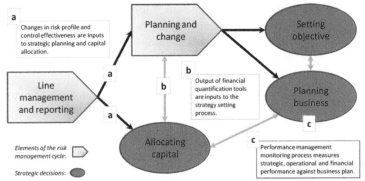

Figure 26 – Information received by management

5.4   Securitization as risk management technique

In recent years, a primary innovation of the secondary mortgage market in the United States is that the risk of default is borne by investors who are many steps removed from borrowers. Traditionally in the US, home mortgages were kept by the local bank (as is true in many countries). If a borrower defaulted, it was the bank that suffered. Thus in previous times, the bank had the incentive to make loans only to creditworthy borrowers. But, in recent years, with an active secondary mortgage market, US lenders were able to securitize or sell their customers' loans to investors. This, in turn, freed up the lender's capital to make more loans. However, the danger in this approach is that there are no longer any gate keepers along the securitization pathway who have an incentive to shut the door on uneconomic loans.

Some believe that the credit crunch arose from the fallout of rising defaults in the US sub-prime mortgage market. In the low interest rate environment, lenders made it easy for those with lower credit scores to obtain credit. These sub-prime loans were then sold on to financial institutions and hedge funds through securitized products on the secondary market. However, as interest rates began to rise and market conditions worsened, these debt packages lost value, and thus banks were left holding assets worth much less than they initially paid. As a result, they became difficult to sell on, and some banks had no other option but to write off some of the debts and close investment funds with exposure to them.

However, there is another explanation for this. The top housing official in the Bill Clinton administration during the 1990s, Henry Cisneros, loosened mortgage restrictions so first-time home buyers could qualify for loans they could never get before. Some feel this was caused by the deliberate US government policies that were brought in to destroy US mortgage lending standards, pillage banks and socialize risk. It begins with the idea, long held among social activists, that US mortgage lending practices prevented home ownership among low income and certain racial groups. Banks and other lenders, following normal and prudent lending standards, were accused of discrimination. The solution: relax lending standards.

One step along that road was the 1970 US Community Reinvestment Act (mandated by President Carter's Community Reinvestment Act of 1977; also, consider President Roosevelt's creation of Fannie Mae as part of the New Deal, forcing banks to lend equally to all geographic areas, regardless of risk). In the 1990s, the Department of Housing and Urban Development mandated that families no longer had to prove five years of income, instead they only needed three, and lenders no longer had to interview borrowers face to face. As housing prices rose, the risk flaws were overshadowed. This gave rise to even greater use of credit, as speculators and buyers piled onto a credit and ownership machine that seemed to offer no risk and guaranteed gains. No-down-payment mortgages or even 110% mortgages were easily obtained. Rising prices, fuelled by easy credit, spilled the housing bubble into the prime US housing market from the sub-prime one. That is not to say that all the funding came via government and regulatory overreach, as hundreds of billions were raised through mortgage-backed securities and other risk-distribution vehicles by private players.

Rating agencies provided poor independent assessments of the default risk.[27]

Therefore, the interpretation of the US sub-prime mortgage collapse as a product of unscrupulous agents and lenders roaming the country in a deregulated market searching for ignorant buyers is overwhelmed by historical facts to the contrary.

As a result of significant problems in the sub-prime market, mortgage lenders in the United States continued to extend loans to ever-more-marginal borrowers because there was a ready party in the secondary market willing to pay a high price for those loans. At best, the debt-rating agencies relied on false information provided by borrowers, which caused them to incorrectly rate packages of mortgage loans. At worst, the agencies perhaps compromised their institutional integrity to earn the resulting fee that came along with an adequate debt rating.

Once the underlying mortgages began performing poorly, the prices of the mortgage-backed securities declined. These securities often served as collateral for hedge funds' margin loans, so as prices declined, brokers demanded more collateral. If the fund was unable to meet the margin call, the securities would be involuntarily liquidated, leading to further price declines that sent more funds head-first into the vicious margin call cycle. After a few high-profile fund disasters, skittish investors began to withdraw capital from all funds with mortgage exposure leading to more liquidation and driving down prices even further. In the midst of it all, credit dried up as financial institutions began to fear the extent of the crisis.

Therefore, the spreading of the originate and distribute banking model led to a separation of those holding credit risks from those monitoring and managing them. Investors assumed that originators would perform proper risk management, but had no guarantee that this

---

27 *"Anatomy of a Train Wreck: Causes of the Mortgage Meltdown" (a chapter in Housing America), By University of Texas economics professor Stan J. Liebowitz.*

would be the case. They put full faith in the ability of rating agencies to draw up risk assessments for instruments that were new. Moreover, some large financial institutions showed a massive concentration of risk, considering the overall size of their balance sheets and capital. While the extensive spreading of risk is generally a stabilising factor at the system level, in extreme circumstances, such as a global loss of confidence, the impact is by definition systemic.

Thus, the global loss of confidence was systemic. There are different schools of thought as to how to address this including amending the system and recognition of securitization as a flawed technique. The years to come will help answer this question.

5.4.1   Conclusion

Risks are assessed at both the inherent and residual levels. The inherent risk is the risk before any controls or mitigating actions are put in place or the risk that the controls and mitigating actions in place all fail. The residual risk assessment takes into account the effectiveness of existing controls and other mitigating actions (for example, transfers of risk). Residual risk assessments are used for capital assessment purposes. The risk management function plays a key role in this assessment.

ERM is the embedded framework designed to be practical, and theoretically consistent, whose main components are fully integrated into the day to day management of risk. The key to ERM is the embeddedness of risk management.

Chapter 6,
Enterprise Risk Management

Luca Paciol:

What is an internal control?

We reply:

o   An internal control is a procedure that reduces the incidence of risk. Control activities may also be explained by the type or nature of activity. These include (but are not limited to): segregation of duties, authorization of transactions, retention of records, supervision or monitoring of operations, physical safeguards, top-level reviews, IT general controls and IT application controls.

Luca Paciol:

What is an Enterprise Risk Management Framework?

We reply:

o   First, we need to understand what is a "framework": it is a conceptual structure providing an underlying hierarchical tool for management which specifies the appropriate principles and standards and detailing the required approach to achieve the desired and necessary outcome. The Risk Management Framework (or Risk Management System) is the strategies, policies, methodologies, tools, processes

and procedures necessary to identify (recognise/
assess/evaluate), measure, mitigate, monitor, manage
and report on a continuous basis the risks, at an
individual and at an aggregated level, to which they
are or could be exposed, and their interdependencies.

6.1 Internal controls

Internal controls include all measures and practices
used to mitigate exposures to risks. An internal control
is a key mechanism used to reduce and manage risks
which is put in place to provide reasonable assurance of
the containment of losses and their volatility to within
acceptable risk tolerance. In this case, the term volatility
refers to the actual and anticipated frequency and
magnitude of changes in the risk exposure.

The objectives of Internal Controls are:

- To promote efficiency and effectiveness of
  operations.

- To help ensure reliability and completeness of
  financial and management information.

- Compliance with applicable laws and regulations.

- To facilitate the safeguarding of assets.

- To help manage risks.

6.1.1 How do internal controls assist in managing risk?

A range of options or risk responses are available to
manage risks, including to avoid, transfer, reduce or
accept a portion or all of those risks that are outside
appetite.

A wide spectrum of control activities

A wide spectrum of control activities can be used to
mitigate the diversity of exposures faced by the

organisation to ensure the company operates within its appetite for risk.

Entity Level Controls (ELCs) provide comfort at a corporate level as well as across businesses. Figure 27 shows that, moving down the spectrum of control activities, there are documented policies that articulate the minimum standards of control to which businesses are required to comply. Lower level control activities to ensure that business risks are within tolerance are also pervasive throughout the organization as well as in categories including supervision and detailed checks. Examples incorporate approvals, authorizations, verifications, recommendations, performance reviews, training, management supervision and segregation of duties. Lower level controls will assist with giving comfort around the aggregate control environment.

Entity level controls	ELCs are high-level controls and are: • Direct (operated by the business), or • Indirect (operated at group level).
Policies	Examples such as: • Risk management and internal control policy • Business protection policy • Human resources policy.
Supervision	Examples: • Authorisation limits • System access control.
Detailed checks	Examples: • Bank reconciliations • Quality assurance procedures.

Figure 27 – A wide spectrum of control activities

The impact and probability of each risk should be assessed on both an inherent basis (before any controls or mitigating actions are put in place or the risk that the controls and mitigating actions in place all fail) and a residual basis (taking into account controls identified and their effectiveness, and other mitigating actions). The impact is a measure of the financial cost to the firm should the risk happen at all. Probability is a measure of the percentage likelihood of a risk happening at all.

Or, said another way, the frequency of an event is how often an event will occur (inherent risk), should occur (risk appetite), and is likely to occur (residual risk). Severity of an event is the cost that would be incurred if the event occurred.

The inherent risk is:

- The risk before any dedicated controls or mitigating actions are put in place, or
- The risk that the dedicated controls and mitigating actions in place all fail.

The inherent risk assessment is based on the assumption that the key controls which are established to fully or in part mitigate the risk are not operating. It does not assume that no dedicated controls are operating.

Thus, residual risk is the value of risk after taking account of any mitigating controls (that is, inherent risk minus current controls). It is also known as the risk remaining after risk treatment.

Where residual risk is outside risk appetite, other mitigating actions (for example avoid or transfers of risk) are available. Risks can also be reduced by improved internal controls.

Avoiding or terminating the risk by adjusting the operations of the firm can be useful so that the risk no longer applies. Termination of the activity is not necessarily possible in the case of mandated or regulatory measures, but the option of closing down an area where the benefits are in doubt is often a real one. Another option is transferring the risk to a third party best placed to mange it, for example by taking out an insurance policy. Some risks, such as reputational risk, cannot be transferred.

Accepting or tolerating the risk is basically the do nothing option, which means the existing management arrangements will be used to handle the results of the risk happening. Thus, these are typically used for low impact risks. Sometimes this response can be just as risky as a more proactive response, particularly in an environment of constant change.

Residual risk assessments are used for capital assessment purposes.

Management of risks

Figure 28 describes the management of risks where residual risks are outside risk appetite or tolerance.

It is necessary for management to use the decision-making process to determine an appropriate response: whether to fully or partially avoid, reduce, transfer or accept.

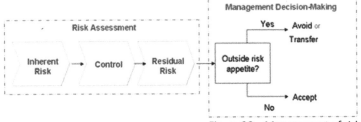

Figure 28 – Management of risks

The risk which remains after the inherent risk has been tempered by the use of internal controls is called the residual risk. In managing residual risk that is outside the risk appetite, the response should be to fully or partially avoid, reduce or transfer. If the risk is within the risk appetite, this is acceptable and no response is necessary. Management can also reduce risks by improved internal controls.

6.1.2   Types of key controls

Controls are designed and operated to respond appropriately to all significant risks in achieving objectives by reducing their impact or probability. Risks are measured according to the probability and adverse impact of the event concerned. The adverse component considers impact or severity while probability views likelihood.

Controls are documented and key indicators are designed, developed and used to evidence the effective operation of internal controls. Key indicators use monitoring evidence to demonstrate that risks are being managed within expected boundaries. Key control testing is used to substantiate the proper operation of minimum standards of internal control.

There are four types of key controls:

- Automated
- Manual
- Direct ELCs which are designed and operated by the line of business
- Indirect ELCs which are designed and operated at a corporate-wide level (these could also be operated by the business area).

In addition, key controls can be classified as preventative or detective. The objective of a preventative control is to prevent an error or risk occurring, for example restricted access over IT systems, segregation of duties and automated data validation within IT systems. A detective control should discover an error or reveal if a risk has occurred. Examples of a detective control include the review of reconciliations and exception reports and the review of security violation report.

In the case of controls, assessments and conclusions are made to assure that risks are being managed within (or beyond) acceptable boundaries. Controls need to be assessed periodically through compliance testing for effectiveness of operation and as a challenge to their validity.

6.1.3   Who establishes controls?

The business and operating areas (fist line of defence) must ensure that they have an effective control environment in place to manage material risks within the stated appetite.

6.1.4   Inherent and residual risk assessments

The inherent risk is the risk before any controls or mitigating actions are put in place, or the risk that the controls and mitigating actions in place all fail. The residual risk assessment takes into account the effectiveness of existing controls and other mitigating actions.

In the control assessment process, control activities are assessed for their overall ability to mitigate the levels of inherent risk to an appropriate level. The control's ability to mitigate a risk is assessed in terms of the adequacy of the control design and the effectiveness of implementation and operation of that control.

Residual risk is the likely impact and probability of a risk, after taking into account the controls in place that have been designed to mitigate the risk to an acceptable level in line with the business' risk appetite. Thus, residual risk is the value of risk after taking into account any mitigating controls (that is, inherent risk minus current controls). It is also known as the risk remaining after risk treatment. Many risk managers consider residual risk to be an expression of the current risk exposure of the business which indicates areas of threat and management focus.

Risk Appetite (in some firms known as risk tolerance) is the level of risk that a firm will accept for an individual risk or in total. The risk appetite can be seen as a series of boundaries authorised by management within which business units must operate. Thus, residual risk must stay within risk appetite.

The day-to-day risks that the organization faces in the operation of its business include the broad categories of corporate, credit, liquidity, market, and operational risks. The broad categories of risk include specific risks. They are identified through risk profiles, risk policies, risk model and committee supervision.

Need to understand inherent risk

Figure 29 shows how both inherent and residual risks should be assessed by considering their impact and probability.

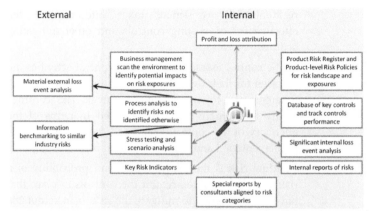

Figure 29 – Techniques for identifying inherent risk

Different dimensions used for the identification of risks

	Product Risks	Firm-wide Risks
Type 1 - Current versus Emerging Risks – The time orientation of the risk identification process.		
Current Risks	Risk Identification process executed primarily by the Product Risks Methodology approach to determine the businesses current product lines' risk exposures.	Existing firm-wide related risk exposures identified through a robust process of management information (for example, top 15 risks) to the Senior Management detailing current risks.
Emerging Risks	Potential product-related business exposures that do not currently exist but may surface at some point in time due to product changes.	Possible firm-wide based exposures that may occur in the future due to changes in the firm or in the environment in which it operates.
Type 2 – Bottom-up versus Top-down – The pathway course of the risk identification process.		
Bottom-up Approach	First line Management identifies product risks relevant to the business of the company and promptly brings these to the attention of the Board, where appropriate.	Firm-wide based Management identifies the risks relevant to the business of the company and promptly brings these to the attention of the Board, where appropriate.

	Product Risks	Firm-wide Risks
Top-down Approach	The Board (or Board Risk Committee) provides supervision through periodic reviews and opines on the identified universe of product risks.	The Board (or Board Risk Committee) obtains assurance, by partnering with Management, by way of supervision, discussion and providing direction, to ensure identification of the Firm-wide related risks relevant to the company.
Type 3 – Internal Influences versus External Factors – The directional stimuli of the risk identification process.		
Internal Influences	Influences driven from within the company that impact products (for example, products which are new, modified or cancelled) and the resultant risk exposures. Internal influences can either impact current exposures or create new risks for the firm.	Influences from within the company that impact Firm-wide type risks (changes in the organisation, processes and systems). Internal influences can either impact current exposures or create new risks for the firm.
External Factors	Factors external to the firm that influence product risks (for example, changes in the insurance market due to competition, regulations) in the environment in which the firm operates. External factors can either impact current exposures or create new risks for the firm.	Effects from the external environment in which the firm operates that impact firm-wide oriented risks (for example, fluctuating economic conditions, changes in legal and regulatory status). External factors can either impact current exposures or create new risks for the firm.

6.1.5   Inherent risks compared with residual risks

Residual risk assessments are used for capital assessment purposes as well as risk reporting. Risk profiles show the residual risk and the condition of the key controls within the business. Risks are measured according to the probability and adverse impact of the event concerned. These assessments are made on an inherent and residual basis.

Figure 30 demonstrates, from left to right, the flow and feedback loop of the risk assessment process.

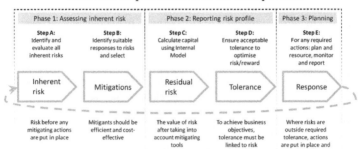

Figure 30 – Risk assessment, profile, reporting and actions process

Key concepts

The firm's risk tolerance for risk and associated minimum controls are set out within the risk management policies. This tolerance is the variance a business will allow in relation to deviations from a target or maximum level of risk exposure, and could therefore be a limit (for example no more than £100m of exposure to AA-rated fixed income securities) or a threshold (for example, invest a minimum of £100m economic capital into insurance risk). The relationship between tolerance and residual risk is the primary focus of risk reporting. For example, in heat maps, green means residual risk is within tolerance, red says residual risk is out of tolerance and amber shows slightly out of tolerance.

Approach

Figure 31 shows how a control comprises those elements of an organization that, taken together, support people in the achievement of the organization's business objectives.

Controls may be adequate and effective to the extent that the risk of the organization failing to meet its objectives efficiently and economically is deemed acceptable. A control is a process or routine put in place by the board of directors, senior management and all levels of staff to provide reasonable assurance that an organisation's objectives will be achieved. It includes all measures and practices used to mitigate exposures to risks that could prevent an organisation from achieving its objectives.

Figure 31 – Definitions and approach

Definitions

Inherent risk

> Risk (expressed in terms of impact and probability) before any dedicated controls or mitigating actions are put in place.

Controls / mitigation, issues to consider:

- What controls are in place?
- Are key controls clearly documented?
- Where control is in place, is management comfortable it is working?
- Are controls efficient and cost-effective?

Residual risk

> The value of risk after taking account of any mitigating controls. (That is: inherent risk *minus* current controls.)

Tolerance

> Tolerance must be linked to appetite, which is the level of acceptable risk to achieve business objective.

Action

> Where risks are not within required tolerance actions are put in place and tracked to mitigate control deficiencies.

6.1.6   Risk responses

There are a number of ways to mitigate a risk, so it is important to understand what mitigation strategies are in place. Those strategies may involve one or more of the four following options (that is, there are four potential responses to the inherent risks a business faces and, in addition, a combination of the four can be used in developing a strategy).

Avoidance:

> Avoidance means getting out of the activities that give rise to the material inherent risk. For example, this may be achieved by removing the planned activity that would lead to the particular risk. Another option to terminate or avoid the risk is to change the scope of the strategic project, so that the risk no longer applies. Examples are:

> o   Disposing of a business unit, product line or geographical segment.

> o   Deciding not to engage in new initiatives or activities that are not part of a firm's appetite for risk.

Transfer:

> Transfer means re-allocating or sharing a portion of the risk in order to reduce it. This can be achieved by transferring the risk to a third party best placed to mange it; for example, by taking out an insurance policy. However some risks, such as reputation risk, cannot be transferred. Examples are:

> o   Insuring against significant unexpected loss.

> o   Entering into joint venture or partnership.

> o   Outsourcing business processes. However, while outsourcing transfers out of the entity some risks (like transaction processing), new

risks are introduced including the risks associated with the management of the contract (such as when a deterioration in service provided by an outsourcer or supplier is not identified, firm fails to consider customer expectations when negotiating outsource or third party arrangements and the company fails to consider customer expectations when negotiating outsource or third party arrangements).

o   Hedging risk through capital market instruments.

o   Sharing risk through contractual agreements with customers or other business partners.

o   Purchasing reinsurance.

Reduction:

Reduction means taking action to decrease the likelihood or impact of the risk. This mitigation of the risk can be achieved by way of on-going actions, tasks or processes to monitor or manage a particular aspect of the risk. A risk is treated by identifying and implementing mitigating actions that address either the probability or impact of the risk, or both, and so contain it at an acceptable level. Controls tend to be the primary way of managing or reducing risks. Examples are:

o   Diversifying product offerings.

o   Establishing operational limits – that is, internal controls.

o   Establishing effective business processes – that is, internal controls.

o   Enhancing management involvement in decision-making, monitoring – that is, internal controls.

o   Rebalancing portfolio of assets to reduce exposure to certain types of loss

o   Instituting business continuity and incident management plans – that is, internal controls.

Acceptance:

> Acceptance means deciding to assume the risk and not take any action. Thus tolerating or accepting the risk is basically the do nothing option, which means the project will use existing management arrangements to handle the results of the risk happening, and if it did crystallise it would be seen as being within appetite. Examples are:
>
> o   Self -insuring against loss.
>
> o   Relying on natural offsets within a portfolio.
>
> o   Accepting risk as already conforming to risk tolerances.
>
> In deciding which of these responses to choose, businesses should consider:
>
> o   The effect the response may have on the risk materialising (that is whether the response will lessen the possibility that this risk will manifest); and
>
> o   Its impact (that is, whether the response will cause the consequences of the risk to be less severe).

The objective of the business is not to eliminate risk; the challenge is to choose control responses that are proportionate to the risks faced, that operate efficiently to bring the inherent risks within acceptable tolerance levels and that do not compromise the achievement of strategic objectives.

Definitions of different risk responses

The objective of risk management is to mitigate risks outside tolerance to the target level. The timescales and resources required to carry out the strategy should also be identified and agreed. There are a number of ways to mitigate a risk, so it is important to understand what mitigation strategies which are best to be used. Figure 32 shows how there are four improvement actions which can be considered: reduce, transfer, avoid, accept. Key actions are monitored and progress reports included in risk reports.

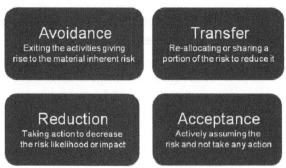

Figure 32 – Definitions of different risk responses

6.2   Risk committees

This section describes the purpose, responsibilities and accountabilities of the risk management committee.

6.2.1   Risk management governance committee

The board's risk management committee provides the board of directors with assurance that key risks significant to the achievement of the company's business objectives are adequately identified, assessed, monitored and controlled. There should be more than one. For example, one possible structure is a senior committee and then subsidiary ones for sectors such as credit risk and market risk.

The risk management committee enables the escalation of significant risk exposures against risk appetite and oversees mitigating actions being taken. Risk management governance is generally delegated at an executive level from the board to the CEO and in turn to an executive committee. Risk management supervision is then discharged by one or more relevant risk management committees/sub-committees to oversee financial and operational risks.

The risk management committee is an integral part of the risk governance framework as it oversees the aggregate risk exposure on behalf of executive management of the firm.

6.2.2 Responsibilities of the risk management committee

The risk management committee should act as the most senior point of management review, counsel and input on the design and assessment of the firm's risk, governance and control.

The risk management committee is responsible for managing the risks inherent in the applicable risk policies under its management (for example, credit and market), and this includes:

- Implementing an overall risk framework for the management of applicable risks throughout the company's businesses.

- Granting approvals, in relation to the management of the risk, as applicable. For example, approving specified types of transactions which are unusual given their size, nature or characteristics and that fall outside a regions' delegated authority.

- Reviewing the aggregate risk profile against appetite.

- Reviewing and monitoring company-wide aggregate risk appetite and tolerances.

- Assessing whether appropriate mitigating actions are in place in the event of an activity or control deficiency taking a business unit significantly out of risk appetite.

- Where applicable, notifying other committees of events or control deficiencies which have taken the firm significantly out of risk appetite and the actions in place to return the company to appetite.

- Reviewing and monitoring significant exposures against the company's risk appetite.

- Reviewing the effectiveness of governance.

6.2.3 Risk management committee's accountabilities

The board's risk management committee should be the final point of senior management review for enterprise-wide control assessments and internal control policies and procedures prior to submission to the board, the audit committee and the senior executive team. The committee should also serve as counsel to the senior executive team on the overall conclusion on the state of control at the bank. At the bank's discretion this can include a number of different types of controls such as: financial process controls (for example, supporting Sarbanes-Oxley or Combined Code requirements in the UK), general entity controls and legal and regulatory compliance controls.

It is important that controls are properly designed (that is, adequate) and operating as specified (effective). It is also important to note that a number of other areas within the bank will be interested in the results of these control assessments (for example, finance, regulatory compliance, audit). All of these should be incorporated into the risk management committees' terms of reference or charter.

6.3 Stress testing and scenario analysis

This section describes the purpose and practice of stress testing.

6.3.1 Introduction to the analysis of stress testing and scenario analysis

One of the key ways to improve the management of risks and crisis is to ensure proper stress testing and scenario analysis is in place. Stress testing and scenario analysis are integral in stimulating crisis situations and assess capital adequacy. Stress tests or scenario analyses are techniques used to validate, supplement, or probe the results of other modelling approaches including considering the impact of various types of crisis on capital.

The stress tests should be tailored to the nature of the FI's business. The stress tests should be designed by taking into consideration the hypothetical, but, also balancing that with what could reasonably be considered as low probability (but, possible) events in the context of the nature of the FI's business. For example the stress test should consider impacts of these hypothetical and possible events, as well as the parallel and non-parallel upward or downwards shifts in the yield curve for all positions or currencies.

The focus of the stress tests is to assess potential impacts on the severity of unusual events. They should not focus on probability, as by their nature we want to consider impacts rather than likelihood (we are not trying to estimate the potential probability of occurrence but rather what would be the result if it did occur). The stress tests incorporate plausible but extreme scenarios to consider possible extreme losses. Or, said another way, the stress tests are designed to test whether or not the FI can absorb significant losses. Consideration should also be given to the nature of stress testing completed by other financial institutions to ensure there was consistency with general practice in the industry.

6.3.2   Objective of stress testing

A key objective of stress testing and scenario analysis is to understand what types of events, factors and variables could cause a survivability risk to the firm. For example, in the case of liquidity risk, the focus is on the concern that a firm, although solvent, either does not have available sufficient financial resources to enable it to meet its obligations as they fall due, or can secure such resources only at excessive costs.

Stress testing methods provide the financial institution with a check of the reliability of risk calculation methods, policies and models in extreme market conditions. The stress tests incorporate plausible but severe scenarios to consider possible extreme losses. Understanding internal or external risks through scenario analysis and stress testing improves the ability of the firm to attribute and allocate (both increases and decreases) capital to mitigate these risks.

Stress testing is a simple form of scenario analysis. Rather than considering the evolution of risk factors over several time steps, stress testing considers changes in risk factors over a single time step. In stress testing in market risk, the time horizon is usually a single trading day, but stress testing can be considered over longer horizons: a week, two weeks, a quarter or even a year. In practice, the terms stress testing and scenario analysis are often used interchangeably.

6.3.3   Stress testing and Basel II

The Basel II Accord refers to stress testing numerous times in relation to each of its three pillars. Nowhere, however, does it attempt to define what constitutes an effective stress test. The accord also makes clear that there needs to be stress testing done in relation to: credit risk liquidity risk in relation to collateral; and market risk. Regulators are also required to ensure that institutions conduct rigorous and forward-looking stress testing to identify factors which could adversely affect the bank. In fact, the entire text of Principle 1 of Pillar 2 is centred on the question of stress testing.[28]

Why do we stress test?

We stress test to assess the vulnerability of a financial institution to adverse events or other external factors such as business cycle risk, and whether or not there is a need to hold additional capital for these risks. Thus, the focus of stress testing is to consider to what extent capital is available to cover unexpected events.

The firm's Basel II documentation should describe stress and scenario analyses completed in the institution's assessment of a particular risk, giving details of the scenarios chosen and the quantitative results. One of the

---

28 *Discussion Paper (DP) 07/7 (DP07/7, dated December, 2007) entitled "Review of the Liquidity Requirements for Banks and Building Societies" (Section 4.5), the Financial Services Authority's (FSA) – UK*

important characteristics of the risk and capital assessments is that it is forward-looking, and includes an element of stress testing. While stress testing is a mandatory Basel II requirement, it must be appropriate and relevant to the business. More specifically, it is acceptable to take a proportionate approach depending on the size, scale, complexity and nature of the bank.

A key objective of scenario analysis and stress testing is to understand what types of events, factors or variables could cause a survivability risk to the firm. In the case of liquidity risk, the focus is on the concern that a firm, although solvent, either does not have available sufficient financial resources to enable it to meet its obligations as they fall due, or can secure such resources only at excessive cost. Stress testing methods provide the bank with a check of the reliability of risk calculation methods, policies and models in extreme market conditions.

The stress tests incorporate plausible but severe scenarios to consider possible extreme losses. Scenario analyses should prudently include a wide diversity of both internal and external environmental factors. Special focus should be placed on how these events or factors can stress the capital base of the firm.

Stress tests are different from back tests. Back tests involve ex post comparisons of the calculated risk and the effectively occurred changes of the value of a portfolio, and assessing differences. Stress testing methods, as well as back testing methods, are essential supplements to advanced types of capital models.

It should be noted that stress testing is different from economic downturn modelling scenarios. The latter is bank-wide in nature and required by Pillar 2 (ICAAP) in Basel II.

6.3.4   Approach to stress testing

A generally agreed definition of stress testing is "stress-testing means choosing scenarios that are costly and rare, and then putting them to a valuation model." In this case, the valuation models will be those used by a bank to calculate its economic capital. The important point to note here is that both the Basel II Accord and this definition call for multiple scenarios. In fact, the current literature makes it abundantly clear that multiple scenarios, of varying likeliness, are required to constitute an effective stress test, and that these tests and scenarios need to be re-run and re-evaluated on a regular basis to accommodate both changes in the bank's asset mix and in future expectations.

This would involve four possibilities:

- Simulating shocks which are more likely to occur than historical observation suggests.

- Simulating shocks that have never occurred.

- Simulating shocks that reflect the possibility that statistical patterns could break down in some circumstances.

- Simulating shocks that reflect some kind of structural break that could occur in the future.

6.3.5 How to execute stress testing

The stress tests for the ICAAP should be of a holistic nature and include management actions. They should include both qualitative and quantitative elements, and must be plausible scenarios which challenge key assumptions. Stress tests should be completed for all the major risk types including the Basel II Pillar 1 risks and Pillar 2 risks as applicable.

Stress tests are different from back tests. The essence of back-testing is to compare actual results with model-generated risk measures; if the comparison is close, the back-test raises no issues regarding the quality of the risk measures/models. Adequate documentation of stress tests should be retained, such as: purpose of test (validate, supplement, or probe the results of other modelling approaches), simulations to capture risks, quantitative results and other information as applicable. Sensitivity analysis ("what if" reviews) of key assumptions should be incorporated into the stress tests as well.

6.3.6   Coverage of stress tests

The use of a broad range of stress tests as a complement to existing risk management tools is beneficial. In many firms, the stress testing of market risk is at a more advanced stage than for credit, liquidity or the general aggregation of risks across a firm. Good practice suggests that stress testing can and should be applied to the full range of material risks that a firm runs, both at business unit level and on an aggregated company-wide basis.

There is little correlation of stress tests amongst risk types, for example as with market and credit risks. In terms of traded market portfolios, stress testing is commonly used for interest rate, equity, foreign exchange, commodity and credit market instruments. Stress testing of credit portfolios and for liquidity or funding is becoming more developed within the industry. For operational risk and aggregation across risk elements, stress testing is at an early stage of development. Stresses based on reputational risk is at a rudimentary stage within the financial services industry, while stresses based on credit risk are typically at a less advanced state of development than those based on market risks. Even allowing for the difficulty of undertaking rigorous credit-risk based stress tests, most firms have only developed methodologies to examine the relatively straightforward and potentially important scenario of the failure of one or more major counterparties.

As for liquidity risk, the ability to stress test is also at a very early stage. Some smaller banks have explored the relatively mechanical (albeit important) process of examining the effect that ratings downgrades might have using a contractual analysis. However behavioural approaches to stress testing liquidity risk in such firms is at an early stage of development. This may be due to the non-linear nature of the availability of liquidity, which makes any kind of rigorous liquidity modelling difficult.

There is a general consensus within the industry that current stress testing (and risk management more generally) is risk specific, often failing to bring together the impact of stresses across different types of risk (such as market, credit, liquidity and operational) and across businesses. Therefore, the stress testing approach executed needs to take both a risk specific and broad firm-wide method to ensure the firm is assessed in both a detailed and comprehensive manner.

6.3.7 Integration within risk management frameworks

Numerical aggregation of the crystallisation of different types of risk is technically difficult and all but impossible when reputational or legal risks are involved. Current stress testing is often undertaken in isolation from other risk factors (that is, very limited stress testing of market and credit risk together, even where portfolios or products have dual market and credit risk characteristics). Generally, the aggregation by firms of stressed risks across a business is at an embryonic stage within the financial services industry. Good practice is for senior management to be presented with a holistic view of the effect of stresses (that is to say, the full implications of extreme but plausible events need to be thought through carefully) and for senior management to take an aggregated view of the implications of stresses. Where formal aggregation is not possible, an informal or impressionistic assessment of the totality of firm-wide effects will still be useful.

6.3.8 Key points in building stress testing scenarios

Loss scenarios need to be used in place of insufficient or incomplete loss data; this does not replace having an effective process for the collection of event-by-event losses above the pre-determined threshold (as defined within the bank's accounting policy) and aggregate/total losses.

The frequency and severity of the scenario analyses must stem from the activities of the respective line of business; all assumptions must be reasonable and defendable, well-supported and documented. Scenarios should be reviewed minimally on an annual basis to ensure they reflect the current risk profile of the business.

External loss event data may be used to supplement scenario analyses as required (and as available). Scenarios should be compliant and documented per the Risk and Capital Measurement Methodology (note: this means detailed documentation, which forms an audit trail that is, the loss scenario template).

6.3.9 Stress testing scenarios – getting started

The loss scenario approach should incorporate both quantitative and qualitative techniques for a better understanding and quantification of the impact associated with major risk for each specific loss type and within the specified line of business. These techniques provide a framework that will allow conversion of one or more descriptive loss possibilities into a measurement outcome – that is, capital.

Loss scenarios should be developed based on events that are, by definition, unusual, infrequent, and often without extensive statistical relevant data. Where a risk exposure has been identified (but, there is little or no internal loss data available), a loss scenario is built by providing a description of an event or particular combination of events that could occur given the worst case scenario in some future state. All corresponding assumptions and risk mitigates or controls for a given risk type need to be identified for each loss scenario.

During this process both the business and risk management (and others, for example, legal, compliance or internal audit) should be consulted for feedback around loss scenario inputs. For capital calculation purposes, the bank should only use loss scenarios that are based on expert opinion, in conjunction with external data, when evaluating the exposure of a business to high severity events. This approach draws on the knowledge of experienced business managers and risk management experts to derive reasoned assessments of plausible severe losses.

Each loss scenario should be revisited at least once a year to validate that the loss scenarios inputs are still applicable in the current business environment (including internal and external factors). To determine frequency, the approach is based on business and risk management feedback, and the question should be asked: "How many events would you expect to occur in a given year; if none within a year, how long a period before you expect an event to occur?" The business should choose a specific frequency. Frequencies are either time or exposure dependent. The frequency should take into consideration the business environment of the industry, the controls or risk mitigants around processes and procedures.

To determine severity, the approach is based on business and risk managements' feedback and the questions should be asked: "What is the average severity per event in this risk category?" and "What is the maximum severity per event in this risk category?" The severity should be stated gross of insurance deductibles. The frequencies should then be validated by various dimensions, including:

- Business volume comparisons.
- External losses.
- Theoretical estimates.

Examples of potential economic scenarios

As part of the capital planning process, the firm should develop and execute economic downturn modelling. This approach examines scenarios and tests whether the firm would be able to manage its business and capital so as to survive, for example, a recession, at the same time as meeting minimum regulatory standards. Thus, the objective is to demonstrate that the firm has sufficient capital and risk management processes to indeed be able to survive a severe economic downturn and continue to meet regulatory standards. To make these scenarios as real as possible, expected management actions should be taken into account during the downturn, reflecting the firm's responses to each stage of the scenarios.

Scenarios can be reviewed in aggregate or by risk type. Consideration should also be given to the nature of stress testing completed by other financial institutions to ensure consistency with industry practice.

The scenarios can be based on hypothetical or classical scenarios, which in some cases have a historic precedent. They can also be descriptive scenarios or use a number of mechanically-designed situations to evaluate the robustness of the calculation method.

These scenarios should be designed to take into consideration hypothetical scenarios, balanced by what could reasonably be considered as low probability but possible events. These scenarios are described in the following table.

Scenario	Description
Recovery	• Global growth slows initially, but soon monetary and fiscal policy stimulates growth. Inflation worries accompany growth upturn. • Easier financing plus possible bailout resolves credit problems quicker than expected. • Equities do well. Supportive macro-economic environment alongside easier financing improves profit outlook. • Government bond yields surge higher. • Risks rise again further out as market excesses and imbalances grow.
Global hard landing	• Credit crunch and high energy prices lead to prolonged period of slow growth. • Some growth but commodities react to slower growth. Inflationary pressures subside, allowing central banks to avoid raising rates. Bonds rally. • Profits fall and companies cut employment. • Lower rates eventually allow global economy to regain traction.

Scenario	Description
	• Equities range-bound, caught between easing of inflationary fears and disappointing growth.
Stagflation	• Continued inflationary pressures driven by high food and energy prices, particularly in emerging markets. Second round wage-pricing power effects seen in developed economies.
	• Tightening bias on monetary policy to fight inflation, elevated risk of policy error.
	• Bond yields rise sharply as real yields begin to normalize.
	• Bad for profits as margins get squeezed.
	• Outlook for equities poor – multiple de-rating continues.
Depression	• Credit crunch worsens, leading to successive financial crises.
	• Long and deep recession as leverage unwinding takes hold. Very bad for equities.
	• Bond yields have significant downside.
	• Currency crisis as reserve currency status is diminished.
	• Deflationary fears surface
Compound depression	• As Depression but compounded by geo-political event.
	• Possible events include civil unrest and terrorism.

6.3.10   Stress testing compared with back testing

Back testing is the ex-post comparison of the calculated risk and the effectively occurred changes of the value of a portfolio. Back testing as well as stress testing methods are essential supplements to value at risk calculations such as variance-covariance method, Monte Carlo simulation and historical simulation. The essence of back testing is to compare actual results with model-generated risk measures; if the comparison is close, the back test raises no issues regarding the quality of the risk measures or models.

Stress testing methods are used in order to check the reliability of value at risk calculation methods in extreme market conditions. Stress testing methods, as well as back testing methods, are essential supplements to value at risk model.

6.4 Risk mitigants

This section describes the different measures available to mitigate risk.

A mitigant is defined as "something causing the item in question to become milder; less in severity." More specifically, a risk mitigant is specific measures used to reduce the extent, nature or severity of a specific event.[29]

6.4.1 Introduction

Risk mitigation, or risk mitigants, are policies, processes, controls or mechanisms whose objective it is to limit negative outcomes associated with a particular risk. One of the key objectives of risk management is to explain how a bank addresses the mitigation of risks. Capital is just one of a number of mitigants available; others include: adequate systems and controls, proper good governance structures, business continuity planning, IT security, compliance reviews, project management, insurance (for example professional indemnity insurance), capital or a mixture of all these. Risk mitigants also include utilisation of credit risk mitigants; namely: collateral, hedging instruments (for example, guarantees and credit derivatives) and asset securitization.

A bank should have comprehensive policies for identifying, measuring, monitoring, controlling and managing the various individual risk types (for example, the various risk types under both Pillar 1 and 2 risk types under Basel II) and to the establishment of limits within which the firm manages its overall exposures.

---

29 *Risk Management in Finance, Dr. Clifford Tjiok, Lehrveranstaltung SS 2005.*

6.4.2 Types of risk mitigants

In fact, where risks are difficult to quantify, the importance of qualitative provisions within the institution increases. Institutions should be mindful that capital is not the only risk mitigant available and that, in many circumstances, risks can be addressed through internal controls. In general, operational sophistication increases as transaction volume increases, primarily due to enhanced automation. Therefore, the relative quality and effectiveness of risk mitigation measures also increase as transaction volumes increase. The net result is that the rate at which operational risk exposure is created decelerates relative to the rate at which transaction volumes increase.

6.4.3 Approach to the risk mitigation

In the risk management process, banks need to assess the extent and ranges of their risks, and record the mitigants they have in place to address those risks.

Generally, under Basel II, total capital is comprised of two components:

- Required regulatory capital – Pillar 1 capital under credit/market/operational risks approaches.

- Other required risk capital – Pillar 2.

Occasionally, there will be a need for capital that is not related to the required Pillar 1 or Pillar 2 capital. This other capital is primarily to fund growth. In this case there is a need to consider how these capital amounts need to link to funding requirements.

The aim of risk mitigation is to reduce the effects of risks which may be realized in the future. This can be done, for example, by requesting additional collateral for credit transactions.

The aim of risk transfer refers to shifting exposures to third parties. This can involve selling the risk position or using hedge transactions (for example, swaps and forward exchange contracts). Risk mitigation can include a mixture of any of the above.

6.4.4 Credit risk mitigation

While banks use credit risk mitigation techniques (including collateral, guarantees and credit derivatives) to reduce their credit risk, these techniques can give rise to other risks that may render the overall risk reduction less effective. These additional risks can include legal risk, documentation risk and liquidity risk. To help mitigate these new additional risks, approved written policies and procedures, or internal controls, should be in place to control the risks.

6.4.5 Operational risk and insurance as a mitigant

One of the opportunities offered by Basel II in respect of capital reduction is the use of insurance as a risk mitigant where a bank's insurance programme is aligned with the bank's operational risk programme. Under Basel II, insurance may only be used as a mitigant where the FI qualifies to use an AMA for operational risk. Banks are allowed to recognize the risk mitigating impact of insurance in the measures of operational risk used for regulatory minimum capital requirements, if they meet qualifying criteria[30]. These criteria include insurance coverage types which are aligned to operational risk loss types and sub-loss types, assessment of the probability of timely payment by insurers, and risk of insurer default.

Subject to meeting qualifying criteria, under the AMA, a bank is allowed to recognize the risk mitigating impact of insurance in the measures of operational risk used for regulatory minimum capital requirements. The recognition of insurance mitigation is limited to 20% of the total operational risk capital charge, after giving effect to Expected Operational Losses offsets.

6.4.6 Insurance outside the FI as a mitigant

In a conceptual manner insurance, as a risk mitigant to operational risk events, is provided by infrastructure entities (which the Bank interfaces with) that have their

---

[30] Risk Management in Finance, Dr. Clifford Tjiok, Lehrveranstaltung SS 2005.

own insurance programmes, namely: payment systems, transaction netting cooperatives, matching facilities, central securities depositories and clearing houses, each with its own paid-up capital, self-insurance, underwritten primary insurance, or re-insurance.

6.4.7 Conclusion

In risk management, banks must assess the extent and range of their risks and record the mitigants they have in place to address those risks. Additionally, the firm needs to include an explanation of how each risk has been mitigated including, where relevant, an explanation of any other specific arrangements (that is, not capital) used to mitigate the risks, for example, insurance, risk management and control structures.

6.5 Management Information required

This section describes the nature, principles and objectives of Management Information (MI).

6.5.1 What is MI?

MI is information that is collected during a period of business activity. It may be about customers, staff, calls, visits, meetings, sales, opinions, parts of a process or predictions. MI is not just numbers. Quantitative data is valuable to any business, but commentary or opinions are also MI and can help provide a comprehensive, balanced view.

Robust MI enables better management of risk, informed decision making process, efficient capital allocation and improved management of earnings volatility.

Different data requirements

The concept of dynamic risk reporting recognises that different stakeholders will have different data requirements depending on their particular area of interest and focus.

Data is key. Figure 33 shows, for example, how a loss database facilitates more informed and accurate decision making, and provides information for capital modelling purposes. In addition, near misses can provide a useful source of data on risks which have materialised and could recur.

Figure 33 – Informed decision making

Risk management and information systems may provide management with more forward-looking information about risk that would allow it to adjust portfolios gradually, and with more foresight, as the economic outlook changes over the business cycle. By being able to measure all quantifiable risks in the organization, management can make more effective, better informed business decisions.

6.5.2   Principles of robust MI

Principle	Description
Accurate	• The correct numbers and commentary contributed by the right people.
Timely	• Available sufficiently quickly after the relevant business activity to enable mangers to act
Relevant and with insight	• Displaying what a manager can do to directly influence an event or issue which needs to be escalated to someone who can take the necessary action. • Providing the required level of insight in terms of figures, commentary and judgment
Consistent	• Consistent on a period by period basis to allow managers to spot trends and make sound decisions • Providing consistent, integrated and comparable view of risk exposure by risk category and business unit • Based on: − Consistent assessment of risks across the

Principle	Description
	company (for example against appetite, policy compliance is integrated with assessment of exposure) — Consistent escalation of risks and issues driven by delegated authority and materiality thresholds — Consistent set of core risk reports is used
Other	• Forward looking and predictive risk MI assist pro-active risk management (for example helps prevent risks from crystallising) • Backward looking risk MI plays a key part in understanding the past (for example allows analysis of trends and causes of events) and informs activity required for systemic risks.

Formal reporting process has four stages

Figure 34 shows how reporting, based on objectives and agreed upon levels of risk, is provided to the required stakeholders to exercise governance within business units and the bank as a whole.

Figure 34 – Formal reporting process

The risk framework includes the identification, assessment, measurement, managing, monitoring and reporting of risks. Gathering data is key for all of the steps and essential to assessment.

6.5.3   Objectives of risk MI

The objectives of risk management information are:

• To manage economic capital allocation transparently and effectively

• To meet regulatory requirements today and tomorrow.

• To embed risk awareness as part of the firm's culture.

- To improve the efficiency and effectiveness of the risk management capability.

- To maintain a complete, single data set, easily accessible, that underpins the risk measurement and reporting.

- To be perceived as world-class by both internal and external stakeholders: to be aspirational.

The dynamic sequence of reporting

Figure 35 demonstrates the dynamic sequence of risk reporting.

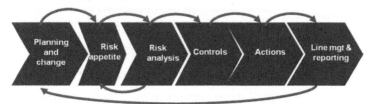

Figure 35 – Dynamic sequence

First determine MI requirements. This is done by determining the key success factors of the organization and the required decisions to be made to support the key success factors. Then, identify what kind of data and information is required to make the needed decisions.

Next gather data. Different stakeholders will have different data requirements depending on their particular area of interest and focus and this may vary across the firm. A distinguishing feature of non-routine transactions is that the data involved is generally not part of the routine flow of transactions and so collection of this data may be difficult.

Then, analyse data. Risk analysis is the systematic use of information (which may include historical data, theoretical analysis, informed opinions, and stakeholder concerns) to estimate the risks. It provides a basis for risk evaluation, risk treatment and risk acceptance.

The cycle of risk management

Figure 36 describes a cycle of risk and mitigants. Where controls and mitigation are deemed to be inadequate to manage risk exposures within appetite and tolerance, documented action plans to improve controls must be designed which include the timescales and resources to carry out these actions. The key objectives of actions will be to: improve control design, improve operation of the control so it functions correctly, or, deliver improvement in a timely manner relative to the risk.

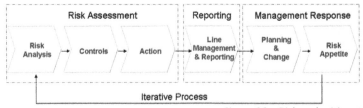

Figure 36 – Risk and mitigants

The risk assessment building blocks of the cycle should provide management with adequate information on risk to inform the decision-making process. The strategic planning process is used to set business targets and recognise the risks to the successful delivery of those objectives.

This is an iterative process as management continues to review its risk appetite over time. For example, where risk appetite exceeds pre-set limits, management will once again complete the computational-type process starting at the beginning with the assessment of risk. In other cases, a new set of controls and actions could result in a more cost-effective approach to managing the risks

Risk Management Framework

A framework is a conceptual structure providing a tool for management.

Figure 37 demonstrates how the Risk Management Framework (or risk management system) is the collection of strategies, policies, methodologies, tools, processes and procedures necessary to identify, measure, mitigate, monitor, manage and report on a continuous basis the risks, at an individual and at an aggregated level, to which they are or could be exposed, and their interdependencies.

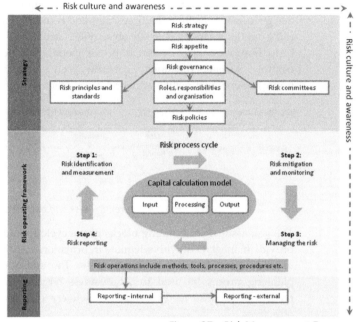

Figure 37 – Risk Management Framework

The risk management framework needs to be embedded across the organisation, which consists of a strong risk culture and management approach. This underpins the firm's overall operation and ensures that business is conducted in a fit and proper manner.

Chapter 7,
Crisis 2008 and Risk Management

Luca Pacioli:

I understand that the Basel III Accord was designed in order to establish a number of new requirements to address a number of deficiencies that were identified in the 2008 financial crisis. What are they?

We reply:

The Basel III Accord establishes new requirements. They include:

o Strengthen global capital rules by raising the quality and quantity of the regulatory capital base and enhance the risk coverage of the capital framework.

o Strengthen liquidity requirements, including required new ratios

o New risk management and governance standards

o Strengthen capital requirements for systemically significant cross-border banks

o Introduce a non risk-based leverage ratio to provide an extra layer of protection

o . Raise capital requirements for the trading book and complex Securitization exposures

o Strengthen the capital requirements for counterparty credit exposure.

7.1   What is a credit crunch?

And what actually happened in 2008?

Until recently, few people had heard of the term credit crunch, but the phrase has now entered common parlance. A credit crunch is defined as "a severe shortage of money or credit", a problem which began a few years ago. Tied to the term of a credit crunch, is the concept of credit risk which is defined as the risk of loss arising from a customer (or counter-party) to a transaction not performing its obligations.

In simple terms, the credit crunch is a crisis caused by banks being too nervous to lend money to us or to each other. In the few cases in which banks will lend, they charge higher rates of interest to cover their risk. Basically, it refers to a specific period when funding from financial institutions is difficult to obtain and hence people also talk about liquidity drying up. During this recessionary time, banks, insurers and investors are very hesitant to lend out any funds and therefore the price of debt products keeps on moving up.

Due to this drying up of liquidity and increased cost of finance, it becomes more and more difficult for companies, institutions and individuals to borrow new funds. This can not only result in halting growth, payment defaults, and increased bankruptcies, but it also can have a devastating ripple effect on the entire economy.

The recent financial crisis and current economic climate means that investors, rating agencies, and regulators are scrutinising the capital and risk management capabilities of financial institutions.

The global financial crisis of 2008-2009 (which included risks related to solvency and liquidity) confirmed that a complex set of rules such as Basel II or Solvency II only stands when they are supported by all three of their pillars. The use of a risk management model that is isolated from the business as a basis for reporting the quantitative estimates is insufficient, no matter how sophisticated the model.

In the case of both Basel II and Solvency II, implementation requires banks and insurers to drive their organization to business compliance, rather than just simply regulatory compliance.[31]

---

31 *"Reading tea leaves under a glass ceiling - Disclosing financial strength" - www.ey.com/insurance, © 2009 EYGM Limited. All Rights Reserved. EYG No. EG0053 0910-1100253 NY.*

In addition, the financial crisis has increased the frequency and severity of insurance claims. In 2007-2009 this was due to losses in FIs following credit and other losses. At the same time the Madoff fraud occurred during the global financial crisis.

7.2 US sub-prime mortgage market

The mortgage melt-down began in the US in the so-called sub-prime mortgage market. When it comes to securitizing mortgages there are two main categories – prime loans which are made to people with good credit records and sub-prime loans which are made to people with not so good credit records (they might have missed a credit card payment or telephone bill or may even be in arrears). When the pool of mortgages is sold they are given a rating: for example AAA for a pool of prime residential mortgages, or BBB for sub-prime, or indeed a mixture of both. This rating is based upon the perceived likelihood of the mortgage being repaid.

Mortgage banks in America made a lot of loans on property to people who could not afford the repayments after the initial discount period of the mortgage had worn off. That meant that the loans the banks had sold to investors started to turn bad. Thus because the loans had turned sour, this meant investors around the globe started to shy away from investing in mortgage backed securities. Without that investment, banks did not have the ability to raise funds and ended up borrowing money off the central banks. Essentially the money markets shut up shop.[32]

7.3 Spreading the risk-securitization of mortgages

This section discusses the nature of securitization and the risks that can occur.

---

32 Web page "The liquidity crisis and the credit crunch". Friday, 18, Apr 2008 12:26 - My Finance.co.uk

7.3.1   What is securitization?

Securitization is executed by creating a more or less standard investment instrument, such as the mortgage "pass-through security", by the pooling of assets to back the instrument. Securitization also refers to the replacement of non-marketable loans and cash flows provided by financial intermediaries with negotiable securities issued in the public capital markets.

Or, said another way, securitization is the process of creating a financial instrument by combining other financial assets and then marketing them to investors. Mortgage backed securities are a good example of securitization.

Banks will often sell these loans off to investors, which is called securitization.

A good example is that of David Bowie. In 1997 David Bowie calculated what he expected his royalty earnings from record sales to be for the next ten years, and decided he would rather have the money now. So he packaged up the rights to his royalty earnings and sold them to investors in the form of Bowie Bonds. Bowie was paid $55m in 1997 for these bonds, and over the next ten years the investors collected whatever royalties Bowie would have earned on his record sales. In effect, this is what banks do with mortgages. They lend out, say, £10m in mortgages. If they were to keep the mortgages on their own books, they would earn (for example) £15m in mortgage payments over 10 years. But rather than do that, the bank instead takes this package of £10m worth of mortgages and sells it to investors for the market price. These investors then receive a return on this investment, in the form of mortgage payments from those who borrowed money from the bank in the first place.[33]

Thus, securitization works by grouping together assets with predictable cash flows or rights to future income streams (such as mortgage or even music royalties – most famously the David Bowie ones described above)

---

33 *Internet page: AndrewLynch.net @ 1 March 2010.*

and turning them into bond-style securities (offering an income stream) that are then sold to investors. It should be noted that while for investors the Bowie Bonds lost some of their value, the basic concept was still sound (and, of course, it was good for Mr. Bowie).

The big benefit to the original owner of the assets or mortgages is that they have inexpensive and expeditious access to low cost capital (or financing) without bank loans.

So securitization makes perfect sense in many situations, including whether a company has substantial capital needs, is seeking to improve its financial performance measures, or if it finds itself constrained by its credit rating. Securitization provides a new way to unlock the income producing potential of the mortgage and to leverage the associated cash flow. This can result in greater returns to the owners of that financial institution, or simply give the FI more funds so they can make more loans to other borrowers and make more money.

Securitization also allows the FI to diversify – finding new sources of funding as well as investment, lowering the overall cost of capital. Essentially the FIs do not have to rely upon savers deposits to lend money and also it carries little risk since the majority of the risk is transferred to a third-party. Therefore securitization is a very attractive option for many FIs.[34]

7.3.2   Credit derivatives

Credit derivatives are often used in securitization transactions. Credit derivatives are privately held negotiable bilateral contracts that allow users to manage their exposure to credit risk. Credit derivatives are financial assets like forward contracts, swaps, and options for which the price is driven by the credit risk of economic agents (private investors or governments). For example, a bank concerned that one of its customers

---

34 Web page "The liquidity crisis and the credit crunch". Friday, 18, Apr 2008 12:26 - My Finance.co.uk

may not be able to repay a loan can protect itself against loss by transferring the credit risk to another party, while keeping the loan on its books.

7.3.3 Risks in securitization

The risks in securitizations are as follows:

Perverse incentives:

A key risk is the flawed incentive structure in the originator-distribution model. When risk of assets is transferred by originators to others, originators have a weaker incentive to carefully distinguish good credits from bad ones. The pursuit of the maximization of provision income can become the overriding goal of originators, while prudent risk selection and monitoring suffer. The most striking example of this trend was the development of the US sub-prime mortgage market. Mortgages were even granted to people without incomes or people with bad credit records.

Rating agency deficiencies:

The securitization approach relied on assessments made by credit rating agencies. Some have charged that problems with conflicts of interest proved to be too strong for some rating agencies. This was exemplified by the phenomenon of so-called ratings shopping by originators at different rating agencies, or alternatively by the gaming of credit risk models by rating agencies in their capacity of advisors to originators.

Increased Interconnectedness:

Securitization can make markets more interconnected. Without securitization, one single party bears all the risk by holding its portfolio until maturity. But when this portfolio is split up into little pieces and sold to investors, more parties are exposed to the same kind of event. This mechanism causes correlations between markets to increase. From a macro-perspective, securitization can actually reinforce the propagation of shocks throughout the financial system. This can especially materialize during extreme co-movements in markets, as was experienced in the market turmoil of September and October 2008.

Evasion of regulation:
Under the Basel I capital adequacy framework, originators had an incentive to move risk off-balance in order to reduce capital requirements. Basel II is a great improvement in this respect, including off-balance entities are considered in the calculation of capital requirements.[35]

7.4   What went wrong and why

This section discusses the lessons to be learnt from the financial crisis of 2008-2009.

7.4.1   Systemic risks of the 2008-2009 global recession

There's an old riddle that goes like this: "What's the difference between a recession and a depression?" "A recession is when your neighbour has lost his job, while a depression is when you've lost your job." Whether you call the 2008-2009 global economic downturn a recession or depression, the bottom line is that it had significant negative implications for most of us.

According to two studies completed by the Financial Stability Forum "a striking aspect of the turmoil (of the 2008-2009 financial crisis) has been the extent of risk management weaknesses and failings at regulated and sophisticated firms." [36]

Key drivers of this collapse included the fact that regulators failed to keep up with the institutional changes that in the last 30 years that have transformed financial markets as well as new style regulatory assumptions. It was assumed that these firms had the technical risk management skills, often expressed in

---

35 *"Securitisation Beyond the Credit Crisis" - Lex Hoogduin, Amsterdam Financial Forum, 28 November 2009.*

36 *'Enhancing market and institutional resilience', April 2008, and 'Follow up on implementation', October, 2008, Financial Stability Forum, Basel (www.fsforum.org)*

their mathematical risk models, to manage exposures properly, over the experience and knowledge of regulators.

In recent years, credit markets throughout the globe have become disintermediated. Instead of banks acting as direct intermediaries between savers and borrowers, the markets took over. A significant proportion of borrowings were packaged into securities that were sliced and sold through a myriad of financial intermediaries. Investment banks were at the centre of this process, taking on massive amounts of debt relative to their capital base (that is, becoming highly leveraged and, thus, incurring great risk) in order to deal profitably in the complex web of markets. Guiding their business model were their mathematical risk models, statistical models which measure the riskiness of their financial operations against patterns of past market behaviour. The firms claimed that they could manage risky markets, and the regulators swallowed that claim. Nothing could have been farther from the truth.

So, how can this be addressed?

First

> Banks must do a better job of understanding and managing their own inherent risks. This issue is discussed throughout this book.

Second

> Regulators must begin to base their approach on the system as a whole. For example, while financial firms are encouraged by supervisors to conduct thousands of stress tests on their risk models, few are conducted by the regulator on a system wide scale. If it is possible to have system-wide stress tests on the impact of Y2K, or of avian flu, why not also test for liquidity or a solvency? The regulators should conduct system wide stress tests of those scenarios most likely to produce systemic stress, such as a 40 per cent drop in house prices. The information gleaned in this exercise should feed into regulatory measures that are likely to be quite

different from those suggested by the risk management of an individual firm.

Third

Financial institutions must be required to undertake more pro-cyclical provisioning, raising their reserves in good times and using those reserves as a cushion in bad times. The rules determining these reserves would be quite different from those governing the regulatory capital that financial institutions are required to hold today. The capital reserve should be an additional charge, not just a buffer or cushion. Since the firm must hold a certain capital reserve to be allowed to operate, it cannot use that reserve to tide it over in bad times. The provisioning requirements should be based on the health of the economy as a whole in order to capture (that is, identify, measure, mitigate, manage and report) systemic strength and weakness.

Fourth

The systemic risks inherent in the misuse of the credit derivatives markets should be addressed by developing common standards and effective clearing. The prevalence of custom-made over-the-counter (OTC) contracts greatly increases the complexity of the market in credit default swaps, a complexity yet further increased by the practice of writing derivatives on derivatives. The introduction of standardised contracts would reduce complexity, and greatly facilitate the establishment of a clearing mechanism. Establishing a clear distinction between regulation of standardised contracts that are readily understood and easily netted (requiring an effective settlement mechanism too), versus complex OTC contracts, would greatly reduce the downside systemic risk.

Fifth

Financial regulation must escape from its present focus on the nature of institutions (for example, commercial banks versus investment banks versus hedge funds) and concentrate instead on the specific functions these institutions are operating within. Regulation must switch from an institutionally defined approach to a functionally defined approach as a vital component of systemic regulation. For national comprehensive regulators, this will be easier to do. In jurisdictions with segmented regulators, like the United States, this will be more difficult.

Finally

Given that a detailed knowledge of the operation and structure of the financial institutions and markets is essential to the effective risk management of systemic exposures, it must be recognised that the required knowledge, if it resides anywhere, resides, at a minimum, with both the regulator and the applicable financial institution.[37]

We all know that the events in the 2008-2009 Global Recession have affected most people throughout the world. In addition to the suggestions for improvements made above, it is important to proactively manage your own risks!

How do you do this? You need to complete your own due diligence by executing your own personal risk management framework. The sequence of steps includes:

1   Determine your risk strategy and risk appetite. What is your attitude to risk? How much risk are you willing to accept? For how much of a required return?

2   Consider the types of risks you are willing to incur and your quantitative risk limits regarding losses.

3   Establish your own methods to monitor and manage your risks. This could include pre-set limits with your broker and established action points.

---

37 *"After the Apocalypse: Lessons from the global financial crisis". Collection of Expert Perspectives. 2008. Demos. Page 24.*

4   Obtain regular information and reports on your risks. Upon receipt these need to be reviewed to ensure your financial objectives are being achieved.

5   Determine and execute any corrective actions as required.

6   Consider all other related matters, such as tax.

7.4.2   The problems with securitization

Securitization changed the old rule of lending money and then managing and monitoring the loan portfolio until the loan matured. In the past, the bank would keep the loan on its balance sheet until the loan was repaid, but all that changed with securitization.

With securitization the banks only needed overnight cash to lend; they borrowed short, wrote mortgages and then sold them on to the securitization industry. The other option, which was even more of a mistake, was to hold onto mortgages after they had been subjected to the alchemy of securitization. Using the magic of AAA credit ratings, they did not have to make a provision against default for all of those wonderful MBSs (Mortgage-Backed Securities, which are basically bonds secured by loans made against a property), ABSs (Asset Backed securities) and CDOs (Collateralised Debt Obligations), they could call them "cash" because as far as the regulators were concerned those things were as liquid as AAA US Treasuries.

Therefore, the banks could borrow very short, take that money and lend it to the home-buyers, thank you very much. Then they took the mortgages, securitized them with the people who bought them often becoming the suckers in the shell game. That mortgages could be written with a loan to value of more than 100% meant the problem would just get bigger.[38]

---

38 *"Ben's Right: Fed Didn't Cause the Crunch, Securitization" (6 January 2010) – Seeking Alpha.*

7.4.3 So what went wrong in 2008?

The credit crunch had its roots in securitization – the parcelling and selling on of risks by banks to other investors. Securitization was meant to disperse risks so that deep-pocketed investors who were better able to absorb losses would share in the risks associated with bank lending. However, in practice, securitization worked to concentrate risks in the banking sector.

There was a simple reason for this. Banks wanted to increase their leverage, to become more indebted, so as to spice up their short-term profit. Rather than dispersing risks evenly throughout the economy, banks bought each other's securities with borrowed money. As a result, far from dispersing risks, securitization had the perverse effect of concentrating all the risks in the banking system itself.

For this reason, securitization has amplified the financial cycle. Accounting rules had a role in the amplification. Banks now have to update the value of their assets based on the current market price: a practice known as "marking to market".

However as banks determine how much they borrow (their leverage) based on their assets, this means that they increase their borrowing in a boom as asset values increase. This causes the boom to go on for longer than it otherwise would. And, in a downturn, banks' assets fall in value. This causes them to reduce their borrowing; this in turn causes asset prices to fall further. This causes busts to be sharper and deeper than they would otherwise be, and this is what occurred in 2008.[39]

7.5 Did it ever happen before?

This section looks at the recent history of financial crises.

---

39 *'Securitisation Amplifies Financial Cycles – And led to the Credit Crunch" - Professor Hyun Song Shin, published in the March 2009 issue of the Economic Journal and summarised in a column on Vox: http://www.voxeu.eu/index.php?q=node/3287*

7.5.1 Introduction

The word globalization is a term well known to most.

Globalization describes the continuing process of integration of the world's many regional economies, political entities and cultures, creating a globe-spanning network of business interconnectedness as well as opportunities. The term is also useful in describing how financial events in a single region can have global implications, both good and bad. Thus, these far off events can result in an impact on your financial position and net.

Let's first discuss various global events and then consider how they can impact us, as well as how these issues can be addressed (that is, how the risks can be managed).

7.5.2 Crisis

A crisis is the manifestation of an uncertain future event which is assumed to result in a loss (immediately or in the future).

7.5.3 The 1980s

It was only after the Mexican debt crisis of 1982 that concrete work on formulating capital adequacy standards began in earnest by the Bank for International Settlements. In the early 1980s, the Basel Committee became concerned that the capital ratios of the main international banks were deteriorating just at the time that international risks, notably those relating to heavily-indebted countries, were growing. This resulted in guidelines being issued for the measurement and assessment of the capital adequacy of banks operating internationally. Thus the agreement, known as the Basel I, set the minimum regulatory capital for banks at 8% of the risk-weighted value of their assets.[40]

---

40 The IDEAs Working Paper Series, IDEAs Francis Smith, Paper no. 09/2006, The Revised Basel Capital Accord: The Logic, Content and Potential Impact for Developing Countries

7.5.4   The third millennium

The recent financial crisis and current economic climate means that investors, rating agencies, and regulators are scrutinising the capital and risk management capabilities of financial institutions.

The global financial crisis of 2008-2009 confirmed that a complex set of rules such as Basel II or Solvency II only stands when they are supported by all three of their pillars. In the case of both Basel II and Solvency II, implementation requires insurers to drive their organization to business compliance, rather than simply regulatory compliance.[41]

In addition, the financial crisis has increased the frequency and severity of insurance claims.

Given the increasing trends of increasing globalization, technology, product and customer and competition sophistication, Risk managers will need to work hard to provide governance and supervision.

---

41 *"Reading tea leaves under a glass ceiling - Disclosing financial strength" - www.ey.com/insurance, © 2009 EYGM Limited. All Rights Reserved. EYG No. EG0053 0910-1100253 NY.*

Chapter 8, What is ahead?

Luca Pacioli:

I've learned much in this question and answer process about risk management, in this regard what can be done to address the deficiencies identified in order to have proper Enterprise Risk Management in place?

We reply:

o It is important that a comprehensive ERM framework is used which looks at the totality of the risk environment that the firm is subject to.

o The Risk Management System is the strategies, policies, methodologies, tools, processes and procedures necessary to identify, measure, mitigate, monitor, manage and report on a continuous basis the risks, at an individual and at an aggregated level, to which they are or could be exposed, and their interdependencies.

Question 2

Luca Pacioli:

What can be done to address the deficiencies identified in Securitization programmes?

We reply:

o Rating agencies need to be independent, with no conflicts of interest, either in fact or as perceived by an independent third party. Also, as required by Dodd-Frank Act in the United States, securitizers need to retain at least 10% of their own issues. This way, the securitization sponsors and originators will continue to have "skin in the game".

Question 3

What can be done to improve the stewardship of risk in banks and insurers?

Luca Pacioli:

We reply:

o   The key point is to try to fix or retain the idea of risk (and return) in the minds of all workers in the enterprise so that it becomes part of normal operations. This includes identifying and addressing all materials risks and ensuring that the proper risk mitigation techniques and management of risks processes are in place. This includes capital adequacy requirements under Basel and Solvency.

8.1   Improving an ERM

This section describes how FIs can establish and improve their ERM.

8.1.1   Fixes required to Enterprise Risk Management

ERM is a holistic view of risk that aims to align risk management with business decision making. It encompasses the culture, processes and tools used to measure, control and manage the universe of risks across the various businesses.

In the financial institutions business, ERM refers to the methods and processes used by organizations to manage risks (or seize opportunities) related to the achievement of their objectives.

Historically, financial organisations have tended to manage risk through specialised departments that identify and manage particular risk. However, each separate department varies in capability and how it coordinates with other departments or functions. A central goal and challenge of ERM is improving this capability and coordination, providing a unified picture of risk for stakeholders and improving the organisation's ability to manage risk effectively.

It is necessary to fully embed ERM in organisations so that risk adjusted profitability and economic capital are considered explicitly when making business decisions.

8.1.2   What should banks and insurers do?

FIs should recognize and measure all the risk and reward trade-offs. This includes understanding their own strengths against the changing nature of systemic risk as well as financial sector sophistication.

The risk-return trade-off means that the potential return rises with an increase in risk, while the opposite is true as well. Or said another way, low levels of uncertainty (low risk and, thus, less capital required) are associated with lower potential returns whereas high levels of uncertainty (high risk, and thus, more capital required) are associated with higher potential returns.

The ability of banks to deal with losses from the sub-prime market, for instance, depends on excellent risk governance, raising senior business leaders' focus on the joint management of risks. Chief risk officers of these financial institutions need to be armed with the analysis needed to spur action and get senior management's and boards' attention. Simply stated, banks will need to go back to the basics of monitoring market credit and operational risk across the enterprise, and progress beyond tick box compliance.[42]

8.1.3   Improving ERM in financial institutions

The credit crunch and 2008-era recession unleashed widespread anger outside the financial sector. And rightly so. Not only did taxpayers have to bail out an industry that is uncommonly well rewarded but the

---

42 *"No bank is an island". IBM Corporation 2008, U.S.A., February 2008. Page 10.*

effects of the credit crunch on the real economy are likely to be painful and prolonged.

Many blame the financiers. Particular attention has been paid to the egregious asymmetry from which the financial sector benefits. High-flying bankers, critics point out, receive large salaries and bonuses when the times are good, and then when the business cycle returns their employers can count on being bailed out by the state. . This mismatch between private reward and public risk is truly unjust. And it is also destabilizing, because it provides the financial sector with the closest thing to a one way bet: heads it wins, tails the taxpayer loses.

Some blame the Anglo-American model of capitalism. For example, a common refrain across Europe is that the crisis was the product of Anglo-Saxon profligacy and the lightly regulated model of finance that fed it. On this view, light regulation, arm's length finance and incomprehensible financial innovation begat irresponsible lending – and the rest of the world suffered from the fall-out.

Some of this is true. Compensation structures in the financial sector appeared to encourage risky short-term behaviour. And financial innovation has been a factor in the current crisis. Securitization, for example, was supposed to have reduced risk by spreading it more widely. However, because originators of loans had no incentive to assess the creditworthiness of borrowers, and credit rating agencies fell short (as Jagdish Bhagwati has remarked) financial innovation did not result in "creative destruction", but in "destructive creation".[43]

As Hyman Minsky has pointed out, it is the prolonged periods of stability that tends to breed instability. Financial crises usually germinate during periods of sustained prosperity when complacency sets in, lending standards weaken and risk aversion falls. In time,

---

43 *"Creative Destruction" is a term coined by Joseph Schumpeter in "Capitalism, Socialism and Democracy" (1942) to describe a process that constantly destroys the current state and creates a new one.*

speculative euphoria develops. At some point, debt exceeds what borrowers can service with their incomes and the speculative bubble bursts. A crisis results in which lenders are forced to rein in credit – with grim repercussions for the real economy.[44]

Or, as stated by Alan Greenspan, in describing the equity markets, it was a time of "irrational exuberance."[45]

8.1.4   Basic principles of establishing an ERM programme

There are two principles around which a firm should build its measurement, monitoring and control processes for the calculation of capital for risk. These are consistent with the spirit and the requirements of the Basel II regulatory framework.

First, risk management is not a stand-alone activity. It is a consistent day-to-day activity that is carried out effectively across the entire consolidated firm, and involves a large number of activities, people and integrated processes. Moreover it is not an exercise whose sole purpose is the calculation of capital. Its goals are complex and integrated into bank management objectives such as creating incentives for better risk management that manifests itself in losses and risk as well as internal control deficiency minimization. This allows the firm to meet the requirements of the use test.

Second, this is a practical activity that should be rooted in the measurement and recording of losses, risks and key control deficiencies, and the development of processes that identify them. Risk management is also linked to other functions that maintain processes which identify losses. All of these processes are inputs into regular periodic reviews such as Risk and Control Assessments and Capital updates.

---

44 *"After the Apocalypse: Lessons from the global financial crisis". Collection of Expert Perspectives. 2008. Demos. Page 66.*
45 *Remarks by Chairman Alan Greenspan, At the Annual Dinner and Francis Boyer Lecture of The American Enterprise Institute for Public Policy Research, Washington, D.C., December 5, 1996, "The Challenge of Central Banking in a Democratic Society"*

8.2 Fixes required for securitization

It is necessary to ensure investor confidence in the securitized instruments. There is a need for a new type of credit rating system not subject to the same inherent conflicts of interest that plagued the previous system. That means in the new system, rating agencies would not be paid by the security sellers trying to sell bonds.

Real estate owners and operators who need funds to roll over debts, buy more properties, or upgrade properties, will have to find ways to borrow money which is not so dependent on securitization. Another alternative would be for securitizers to retain at least 10% of their own issues, taken from the lowest-ranking tranche.[46]

8.2.1 Managing risks

According to an article in the Financial Times by the six CEOs of the six major Canadian banks, the three main causes of the 2008-2009 financial crisis were as follows:

1 Excessive leverage in the banks and investment dealers.

2 Lack of common standards for the quality and level of capital.

3 Weaknesses in risk management and liquidity management.

Regarding the last point, any earlier poor risk management practices must be addressed.[47]

8.3 Fixes required for rating agencies

Ratings made by external credit rating agencies will increasingly be driven by assessments of the quality of a firm's overall risk management. Assessments are pushing a higher standard by:

---

46 *Securitization Hibernation - Oct 1, 2008 12:00 PM, By Anthony Downs - Web page: http://nreionline.com/commentary/money/securitization-hibernation/*
47 *"It is time to press on with bank reform", by Ed Clark, Financial Times, UK, 22 April 2010, page 13*

- Focusing on the rigour of a firm's overall risk management approach, its appropriateness to the business and its impact on business decisions.

- Driving improvements in risk management in relation to greater public disclosure on the quality of risk management.

- Establishing benchmarks against which individual companies will be evaluated and differentiated from one another.

8.4 Changes to Basel and Solvency

Under the Basel II requirements, regulators require banks to have a robust process in place to identify, measure, monitor and control risk.

Basel II raised the standard by increasing the focus on:

- A principles-based approach delivering outcomes in real terms rather than prescribing a detailed process.

- Incentivising firms by rewarding them for using modern and appropriate risk management practices.

- The Use Test – demonstrating that risk management judgments are key to the Firm's management.

- Not just capital, but also the qualitative standards used by the business (that is, the operation of the risk management and control framework).

- Quality risk management which is important to customers and other stakeholders.

8.4.1 Recommendations to governments

In light of the above, governments should consider the following improvements to their stewardship of banks and insurers:

- Raise capital requirements.

- FI should have substantial liabilities that can be converted into equity or treated just as if they were equity, in the case of a bankruptcy or major restructuring procedure.

- Capital requirements should be counter-cyclical. (That is, capital buffers of resources build up during economic expansion periods in order to absorb losses without triggering or amplifying an economic downturn.)

- FIs should hold a large stock of assets that are easy to value by lenders of last resort. This would also provide a source of liquidity where required.

- Change performance evaluation and remunerative incentives within FIs. The managers of failing institutions should receive bonuses in shares they cannot sell until a number of years later. Procedures for claw-back should apply where they want to cash out early Otherwise, it is too easy to gain from strategies with a high probability of blowing up.

- Impose much higher capital and collateral requirements against trading in derivatives. And, all such activities should be moved on to exchanges.

- Improve the quality of information available about FIs. To do this, change the payment system for rating agencies. Since they provide a public good, they should be funded by a general levy.[48]

8.4.2   Crisis impacting a single entity

A crisis impacting a single entity is an event or situation which threatens the continuity of the business or can seriously affect its reputation. One of the key objectives of Basel II and Solvency II is to assist in managing crisis.

For example, Solvency II can improve a company's ability to strike a more sustainable balance between risk and reward and provide comfort for a firm's board and external stakeholders that risks are being actively

---

48 *"Why cautious reform of finance is the risky option". By Martin Wolf. Financial Times. 28 April 2010. Page 13.*

controlled. Lessons from the credit crunch crisis provide a clear indication of the value of such a process. Boards that could draw on timely, reliable and forward-looking analysis of their firm-wide exposures were generally able to anticipate the looming crisis and withdraw before they suffered major losses. To realise these benefits, many insurers will need to develop a more systematic approach to governance and risk management.[49]

Under Solvency II's Pillar 2, in addition to the standard capital requirements of Pillar 1, insurance supervisors have the right to intervene (for example, require additional capital) when a company faces a crisis that might harm policyholders. The same is true for Basel II's Pillar 2.

It is important to remember that the proper management of a crisis is the responsibility of the executive management. This includes ultimate crisis management decision-making authority, providing strategic guidance where necessary and reviewing the management of incidents following their conclusion.

8.5   Still too big to fail?

In a recent newspaper article, the concept of preventing "too big to fail" was exposed as being very difficult for regulators to address. In the article, the author said many small banks are exposed to the same risks as a single large bank and for their smaller brethren this may be even harder to resolve. That is, the Lehman's collapse froze credit markets not because Lehman was so big but because so many financial groups – big and small alike – were interconnected, over-leveraged and exposed to risks nobody understood.[50]

Therefore, wherever possible, regulations for FIs must be globally as consistent as possible.

---

49 *Insurance, Gearing up for Solvency II, Making Solvency II work for the business, September 2008 - 2008 PricewaterhouseCoopers.*
50 *The Financial Times, London, UK, 22 March 2010. "Designs that ignore the wider terrain". By Clive Crook. Page 11.*

And consumers of financial products must use the old maxim "caveat emptor", that is, buyer beware!

8.5.1 Too big to fail – its future

Have we in western capitalist societies lost our appetite for risk?

The efforts by various governments to intervene in the financial markets and rescue financial institutions from the 2008-2009 global depression has been deemed a positive thing by most people. The driving principle offered is that the large investment banks and commercial banks are too big to fail.

However, a key premise of capitalism is the taking of risks, including the possibility of all-out failure. Capitalism is about potentially reaping rewards by taking a corresponding amount of risk. But, if governments continue to choose to treat market participants like consumers who continually expect that some type of safety net will be provided for every transaction, then this will have serious and negative impacts for the future.

In our view, we should allow big banks to fail because market stability requires it.

A major concern here is that we, in western capitalist societies, have lost our appetite for risk. We have regulated risk away to the point that we are now scared to let any large financial institution fail.

However, what's wrong with FIs going through a natural life cycle of cradle to grave?

Let us not forget that, in the case of an FI failure, there would, in most cases, be many other FIs who could come in and buy up the deposits, performing loans, deposit instruments and insurance contracts.

In our opinion (and we agree with other financial commentators) these governments erred in believing that the failure of one bank amounts to market failure. This is not the case.

In 2007 and 2008, were the financial markets of the major OECD countries and others really in any danger of a complete collapse and melt down?

In the opinion of the authors, we would say no!

While there were fewer lending activities during this period, as well as increased unemployment and a small amount of contraction in the economy, there was by no means a wholesale economic meltdown.

While you may be concerned about your job and, therefore, not keen to borrow, that does not automatically mean that the markets and globally economy is collapsing.

Governments need to understand that retaining the possibility of FI failure leads, in the long term, to more efficient and effective financial markets.

Regulators and their governmental masters can put stability back into the markets by allowing, and requiring, that market participants pursue risk and live or die by risk.[51]

In this way, because financial institutions know that they could go under, they will take the management of risks much more seriously.

8.6 Can it ever happen again?

This section considers the actions that institutions and individuals can take to protect themselves from future risk.

8.6.1 Lessons from the Icelandic Bank debacle

Caveat emptor is also an important lesson from the events in Iceland over the last couple of years.

In early March 2010, Icelanders, by way of a national referendum, resoundingly rejected a plan to reimburse overseas depositors after the failure of an online Icelandic bank two years earlier. A whopping 93% of Icelanders rebuffed a government push to reimburse

---

51 *"Banks 'Too Big to Fail'? Wrong" – Business Week - By Alton E. Drew – web page: MyTake February 18, 2009*

Britain and the Netherlands of US$5.3 billion from the October 2008 collapse of an Icelandic internet bank. At the time of the banking collapse in 2008, the failure led Britain and the Netherlands, the two nations where the bank had foreign depositors, to step in and partially pay back billions of sterling and euros lost by their citizens, who were lured in by the bank's high interest rates.

It was also a vote against government officials, analysts said, whom many Icelanders blame for allowing those years of excess to take place. A full repayment to foreign depositors would have amounted to more than $100 per person per month in Iceland for up to eight years. It would have come at a time when unemployment has shot up in Iceland due to a lingering and deep recession. The result of the vote underscored the risks of global online banking schemes.[52]

The Icelandic financial debacle resulted in the ruin of its three key banks including Glitnir, Landsbanki and Kaupthing, as well as Landsbanki's online Icesave brand.

But, how could a tiny fishing nation, with a population of approximately 300,000, decide, around 2003, to re-invent itself as a global financial power? In 2003, Iceland's three biggest banks had assets of only a few billion dollars, about 100% of its gross domestic product. Over the next three and a half years they grew to over $140 billion and were so much greater than Iceland's GDP. that it made no sense to calculate the percentage of it they accounted for. It was, as one unnamed economist put it, "the most rapid expansion of a banking system in the history of mankind."

At the same time, in part because the banks were also lending Icelanders money to buy stocks and real estate, the value of Icelandic stocks and real estate went through the roof. From 2003 to 2007, while the US stock market was doubling, the Icelandic stock market multiplied by nine times. Reykjavik real-estate prices

---

52 *"Icelanders reject full repayment to British, Dutch caught in bank collapse". By Anthony Faiola, Washington Post Foreign Service, Monday, March 8, 2010.*

tripled. By 2006, the average Icelandic family was three times as wealthy as it had been in 2003, and virtually all of this new wealth was in one way or another tied to the new investment-banking industry.

"Everyone was learning Black-Scholes" (the option-pricing model), says Ragnar Arnason, a professor of fishing economics at the University of Iceland, who watched students flee the economics of fishing for the economics of money. "The schools of engineering and math were offering courses on financial engineering. We had hundreds and hundreds of people studying finance." This in a country the size of State of Kentucky in the USA.

But, in the autumn of 2008, Iceland, as a nation, effectively went bust.[53]

So what went wrong?

First, there was insufficient effective risk management in place. In addition, risk models, to a large extent, drove the hyper growth with little acknowledgment that in fact it was a house of cards (and, ready to collapse at any time).

These risk management models had significant deficiencies. They had poor input data, were incorrectly designed, had flawed assumptions and bore no resemblance to the real world. These were serious deficiencies in the risk models.

It reminds us of a not-so-old saying: statistical and other models (including risk models) are like bikinis – what they reveal is suggestive, but what they conceal is vital. So said the late Aaron Levenstein at New York's Baruch College.[54]

The implications to depositors in numerous foreign jurisdictions (like the UK and those in continental Europe) was financially devastating to Iceland. It will take many years for the tiny country to recover.

---

53 *"Wall Street on the Tundra", Vanity Fair, by Michael Lewis, April, 2009.*
54 *"Lessons from the Collapse of Bear Stern", by John Cassidy. Financial Times (London). March 15, 2010. Page 11.*

Once again, consumers must execute an element of their own risk management frameworks. If the returns from tiny Iceland didn't make sense they should have "hit the brakes".

8.6.2 Improving the art and science of risk management

Irrespective of the future role of government in regulating financial institutions, and the regulatory fixes or solutions they decide or do not decide to implement, the effective management of risk must be a core competency within the financial institutions.

8.6.3 What can people do to protect themselves?

Regarding the global financial services turmoil of recent years, management of the various financial institutions (especially risk management) must acknowledge their guilt.

And consumers of financial products must use the old maxim caveat emptor.

How can a consumer do this?

Consumers must be well-informed and use their common sense. They must be prudent. Of course, like the old saying, "common sense isn't very common".

That said, consumers should read as much as they can in the general and financial media about events that are occurring worldwide.

From now on, the key is to always to identify, assess, measure, monitor and manage the current and potential future risks.

In addition, purchasers of financial services must use prudence in their selection of institutions and products.

8.6.4 Increased regulation – potential regulatory changes

While making predictions is inherently difficult to do with any meaningful level of accuracy, it is reasonable to assume that, in the future, there will be increased regulatory requirements.

To address the recent global financial crisis, a number of regulatory fixes or solutions have been suggested including:

1 Large increases in capital to be held by financial institutions.

2 Separation of standard (for example, retail and small business banking) and complex capital markets ones (for example, investment banking, proprietary trading and high yield operations). The same would be true of insurers.

3 Creation of a systemic and global regulator.

4 A too-big-to-fail tax for financial institutions.

5 Taking a back to basics approach with a strong, independent and intelligent financial regulator.

Of course, the quick and easy solution for regulators is to require financial institutions to set aside larger amounts of capital. The problem with this approach is that it does not always result in a sufficient level of analysis of the sources of risks (that is, root cause analysis) to help ensure that all exposures are properly identified, measured and capitalized.

Regarding point 2: some regulators have already started the process of separating the banking and insurance activities that support average consumers from those that are very complex and riskier. Essentially, this approach is moving back to a Glass-Steagall type environment (the Glass-Steagall Act in the US arose in 1933 and was an act to separate investment and commercial banking). This is now happening in the United States.

Regarding point 3: some suggest the introduction of a multi-jurisdictional regulator. However, creation of this is highly unlikely as history provides many examples of the inability to obtain worldwide political consensus in many subject areas (such as nuclear proliferation and the environment). Therefore, it is unlikely that serious global financial regulatory consolidation is going to happen. Thus, the bottom line is that there will continue to be many regulatory agencies (domestic, foreign and multi-national) and it will continue to be difficult to get them all to play nice with each other. Multiple regulators in both the same country and for international political entities (such as the European Union) will probably, unfortunately, continue to be in place (that is, a lack of an international super agency).[55]

Therefore, regulatory arbitrage by banks and insurers will continue as well. But regulators should continue to be vigilant in this regard. (Regulatory arbitrage or regulatory shopping is sometimes used to describe firms structuring or relocating transactions to choose the least burdensome regulator.)

It is also key that regulators complete their detailed regulatory reviews and audits with a view to ensuring that they understand the nature of the business in which the FI operates, and to understanding the key risks, including transactions of a complex and sophisticated nature.

Regarding point 4: some are suggesting a too-big-to-fail tax for financial institutions. This would provide a source of financing in the case where an FI is unable to meet its commitments.

Regarding point 5: in addition to any of the other suggestions, or simply by itself, the back to basics approach would be a good regulatory fix which would ensure that a strong, independent and intelligent financial regulator existed who would refuse to get snowed by bankers' or insurers' jargon and their impenetrable methodologies and models.

Improved transparency of activities within these firms (which regulators should mandate) and more robust risk management and governance practices are essential prerequisites as well.

---

55 *Eight questions for Felix Salmon, Jul 25th 2009, 17:25 by The Economist, Washington (web page).*

Chapter 9, Conclusions

9.1   Understanding the challenges

Risk management continues to advance into the mainstream of business life. Banks now associate risk management much more with innovation and striving to enable sources of competitive differentiation.

Development of future standards on risk management should assist when measuring and managing risk to ensure the adequacy of capital.

Banking business models today are more volatile and more complex than even a few years ago. Firms are trying to discover where profitability and growth will come from in the future. To manage the business from now on, they need greater risk management capabilities. They need to be able to look at different markets, customers and product lines in a more sophisticated manner (such as risk-based capital measures) and ultimately to be able to adjust the approach as they try to take business forward in a more complex environment.

Risk management has a higher priority today. Many companies now consider their risk divisions to be key management functions that help them deal with marketplace volatility and organizational complexity.

As banks innovate and compete, by default they must take on more risk. So the only way for them to succeed in this highly innovated environment is by having better risk management capabilities.

Senior management is becoming much more aware of the need to put measures in place around individual understanding and engagement and the overall level of risk awareness in organizations. As a result, there is often a need for training to be put in place to ensure that all employees understand their specific roles in managing risk in the organization.

In the wake of the recent financial crisis, banks are looking to transform the way that they manage risks. Pressures on margins, the high cost of technology and burgeoning regulation mean that firms are searching for competitive differentiation by moving from compliance to performance and adopting more effective and efficient risk management practices. Risk-based capital techniques help to achieve this. Culture and collaboration are also critical success factors.

Chapter 10,   Glossary

Term	Description
Absolute Risk	Also called "inherent risk". Risks are assessed at both the inherent and residual levels. The inherent risk is the risk before any controls or mitigating actions are put in place or the risk that the controls and mitigating actions in place all fail. The residual risk assessment takes into account the effectiveness of existing controls and other mitigating actions (for example, transfers of risk). Residual risk assessments are used for capital assessment purposes.
Adequacy	The adequacy of control design – That is, how well the control should work in theory (if it is applied when it should be and in the way intended by its designer). A control is either well designed - adequate to mitigate the risk, or it is badly designed – it is inadequate. If a control's design is inadequate there is no need to review effectiveness as no matter how well it is operated it will not perform the intended risk mitigation.
Advanced Internal Ratings Based Approach (AIRB)	This method allows the use of internal bank data, including probability of default (PD), loss given default (LGD) and exposure at default (EAD), in order to calculate risk-weighted assets for the purposes of the Basel II capital calculation.
Advanced Measurement Approach (AMA)	The Advanced Measurement Approach (AMA) is a more sophisticated and comprehensive method for calculating operational risk capital which incorporates the characteristics of the area's risk profile. The methodology often uses both quantitative (e.g. loss history or scenarios) and qualitative information (for example, internal control structure status) to arrive at operational risk capital. Use of AMA for regulatory capital purposes is subject to supervisory approval but is sometimes used earlier in calculating economic capital.
Aggregation	The addition of value at risk results to produce an overall total value for economic capital. Risk aggregation is a quantitative measure that is derived

Term	Description
	from the consolidation of different risk types and their respective measures. Different types of risks are analysed using different assumptions, methodologies and measures depending on the appropriateness for the specific risk type. Risk aggregation converts the different measures for all the different types of risks into a single value.
Appetite	See Risk Appetite and Risk Tolerance
Asset-Liability Management	This is the matching of the amounts of assets and liabilities by term and interest rate type. Financial institutions carry out asset-liability management when they match the maturity of their deposits with the length of their loan commitments to keep from being adversely affected by rapid changes in interest rates.
Assurance	The risk-based review of systems and controls and subsequent provision of an opinion as to whether the internal control framework is in place, operating effectively and sustainable. Assurance may be provided by Internal or External Audit (3rd line of defence), Risk Departments (2nd line of defence) or business areas (1st line of defence).
Attributed Capital	Attributed capital refers to the capital directly assessed and assigned to a production or infrastructure reflecting the risk managed by the respective group.
Bank for International Settlements (BIS)	Is a financial support mechanism for the benefit of the various central banks. It is the institution that provides the secretariat for the Basel Committee on Banking Supervision (BCBS) and hence the work on the Basel Capital Framework. The BIS is an international organisation, which fosters cooperation among central banks and other agencies in pursuit of monetary and financial stability. Its banking services are provided exclusively to central banks and international organisations.
Basel Committee on Banking Supervision (BCBS)	Is the Committee charged with international safety and soundness issues for banks including the Basel Capital Framework. The Basel Committee formulates broad supervisory standards and guidelines and recommends statements of best practice in the

Glossary

Term	Description
	expectation that individual authorities will take steps to implement them through detailed arrangements - statutory or otherwise - which are best suited to their own national systems.
Basel II (or Solvency II) Capital Requirement	In the context of the Basel II (or Solvency II) regime, it is the unexpected loss amount (or value-at-risk (VaR)) measured over one year to a stated (for example, 1 in 1,000) confidence level taking into account diversification and risk mitigation in place. The Capital Requirements may be derived using either an approved internal model or a standard approach, but in both cases it is based on the principles of economic capital and economic value.
Basel III Capital Requirement	These are new capital requirements established in order to strengthen global capital and liquidity rules, promote a more resilient banking sector and improve risk management and governance.
Business Risks	The day to day risks that the organization faces in the operation of its business including the broad categories of corporate, credit, liquidity, market, and operational risks. The broad categories of risk include specific risks. Business Risk is the risk arising from the adoption of the firm's agreed strategy and its implementation at business unit level.
Capital adequacy	The measure of the sufficiency of a bank to meet its business and regulatory obligations.
Capital Adequacy risk	The risk that the firm has insufficient capital resources available to meet its regulatory capital requirements.
Capital Deficit	Capital Resources (Available) is less than Capital Resources Requirements
Capital Ratio	The ratio of an institution's own capital resources to its risk weighted assets.
Capital Requirements Directive	The regulations on capital required in the EU.
Capital Resources (Available)	Capital Resources (Available) = Total Capital = Tier 1 capital + Tier 2 capital + Tier 3 capital (under Basel II)

Term	Description
Capital Resources Requirements	Capital Resources Requirements = Pillar 1 + Pillar 2 (under Basel II)
Capital Surplus	Capital Surplus = Capital Resources (Available) is greater than Capital Resources Requirements
Compensating (Internal) Control	Alternative monitoring controls which compensate for weaknesses in monitoring and procedural controls. Compensating controls are typically detective in nature and may reside elsewhere along the process flow. Simply stated, they are an adequate second choice when the preferred controls are not working.
Confidence level	The critical point on the probability distribution of liability amounts (or some other quantity) before which the required capital is adequate to cover losses.
Control (internal) activities	Policies and procedures that help ensure management directives are carried out. They help ensure that necessary actions are taken to address potential (perceived) and real risks that would impact on the ability to achieve the entity's objectives.
Corporate Governance Framework	Corporate Governance consists in three principal elements: • A pervasive culture and management approach which underpins the overall operation of the Group and ensures that its business is conducted in a fit and proper manner. • A Group-wide governance framework which prescribes constraints in the form of rules, processes, organisation and responsibilities, and within which management operates. • The execution of that governance framework through the fulfilment and observance of its rules, processes and roles so as to ensure that any matters flowing through the framework fully comply with its requirements
Country of Risk	The country of risk is the risk that the counterparty/obligor can not pay its obligations because of cross border restrictions on the convertibility/availability of a given currency. It also includes the political and economic risk of a country.

Term	Description
	The key is to look through the country of residence or domicile and focus on the country of risk. The Country of Risk is the primary country within which a sovereign risk event would need to take place in order to prevent repayment of the facility. For example, if the sole cash flow of a UK company was deriving from an asset in Russia generating cash onshore, this would be viewed as Russian sovereign risk since foreign exchange controls in Russia would prevent the repatriation of profit and the repayment of the facilities. Likewise, if a facility to an Algerian entity was fully insured with a Swiss insurance company this would be viewed as Swiss sovereign risk since, even in the event of failure of the Algerian counterparty, it would be a Swiss sovereign risk event that would prevent us from getting repaid.
Credit Risk	The risk of financial loss arising from default of a customer or counterparty to which the firm has directly provided credit, or for which the firm has assumed a financial obligation.
Design Deficiency (of control)	A deficiency in design exits when (a) a control necessary to meet the control objectives is missing or (b) an existing control is not properly designed so that if the control operates as designed, the control objective is not always met.
Design Effectiveness (of control)	A control is considered properly designed so that when performed properly, the relevant risk is mitigated. The effectiveness of control operation refers to the way in which the control is operated in practice (that is, if it is always applied the way it is intended). There are two mutually exclusive alternatives: either the control is operated as designed and documented (effective) or it is not (ineffective). Assurance as to the effectiveness of controls can only be gained by evidence of their continuing operation.
Detective Controls	Detective controls are designed to identify and correct errors that have already occurred.
Economic Capital	The capital estimated by management to be required against potential losses based upon a quantitative

Term	Description
	assessment of the risks and other capital needs of individual businesses and activities. It is distinct from regulatory capital which is the capital requirement imposed by regulatory bodies. Economic capital can also be defined as the unexpected loss protection that various constituents utilize to ensure the bank will be able to operate as an independent going concern in periods of "worst case" loss scenarios.
Embedding	The process where risk management is not viewed as a separate process or activity, but as a competency that is embedded throughout the firm and supported by its organizational structure. This results is the inculcation of a strong risk culture throughout the company with concurrent risk-related roles and responsibilities identified and accepted. This key competency enhances the firm's ability to manage uncertainty and volatility.
Emerging risks	Are defined as those risks that are at an early stage of becoming known and/or coming into being, and are expected to grow greatly in significance.
Enhanced Capital Requirements	(ECR) A realistic assessment of capital needed plus additional capital set aside based on the results of stress testing.
Enterprise - wide Risk Management Framework	To start with, a "framework" is a conceptual structure providing an underlying hierarchical tool for management which specifies the appropriate principles and standards and detailing the required approach to achieve the desired and necessary outcome. A framework is like a frame of a picture or even more specifically a system of building scaffolds used as the structural guide to construct something. The Risk Management Framework (or Risk Management System) is the strategies, policies, methodologies, tools, processes and procedures necessary to identify (recognise/ assess/evaluate), measure, mitigate, monitor, manage and report on a continuous basis the risks, at an individual and at an aggregated level, to which they are or could be exposed, and their interdependencies.
Expected Loss	Expected loss refers to most likely or average loss in a given year for a given business unit and loss type. It is

Term	Description
	the anticipated loss that arises based upon current information at a specified degree of statistical confidence.
Exposure at Default (EAD)	Is the expected total exposure of the facility when a default of the obligor occurs.
Fungibility of capital	The transferability of capital resources across legal entities.
General Insurance	Or non-life insurance policies, including automobile and homeowners policies, provide payments depending on the loss from a particular financial event. General insurance typically comprises any insurance that is not determined to be life insurance. It is called: • Property and casualty insurance in the U.S. • Non-Life Insurance in Continental Europe. • General Insurance in the UK. In the UK, General insurance is broadly divided into personal lines and commercial lines.
Governance	The decision-making processes of the corporate governance structure which encompasses the overall risk management framework, comprising a set of inter-linking delegated authorities, group policies, supporting Risk Management committees and key supervision and Risk roles with defined role profiles and specified responsibilities. Based on objectives and agreed upon levels of risk, reporting is provided to the required stakeholders to exercise governance within business units and the bank as a whole.
Group Risk	The possibility that a risk that initiates in one or more of the corporate group's companies but could potentially spread and negatively impact one or more of the other branded entities within the group companies.
Hedgeable Risks	A risk that a party can reduce their exposure to by purchasing a hedging instrument or transferring the exposure to a willing, rational, diversified counterparty in an arms' length transaction under normal business conditions (for example, securitization, derivatives such as options and futures).

Term	Description
Home country	The country where the head office of an international bank and where its lead regulator is located.
Home supervisor	The local regulator in the jurisdiction in which an FI's Head Office is domiciled and licensed to perform its activities (home country).
Host country	The country where a subsidiary, branch or other legal entity of an international bank is located, if different from the home country.
Hybrid capital	Capital instruments having varying combinations of both debt and equity characteristics
IFRS	International Financial Reporting Standards
Impact and Probability	The impact and probability of each risk should be assessed on both an inherent basis (before any controls or mitigating actions are put in place or the risk that the controls and mitigating actions in place all fail) and residual basis (taking into account controls identified and their effectiveness, and other mitigating actions) basis. Impact – This is a measure of the financial cost to the FI should the legal risk happen at all. Probability – This is a measure of the percentage likelihood of a risk happening at all.
Inherent Risk	The inherent risk is: • the risk before any dedicated controls or mitigating actions are put in place or • the risk that the dedicated controls and mitigating actions in place all fail The inherent risk assessment is based on the assumption that the key controls which are established to fully or in part mitigate the risk are not operating. It does not assume that no dedicated controls are operating.
Insurance Risk	The risk arising from the inherent uncertainties as to the occurrence, value and timing of insurance liabilities and the risk of adverse variance from key insurance assumptions leading to fluctuation in claims experience and loss.

Glossary

Term	Description
	The key components of insurance risk include: • Underwriting Risk: arises out of unexpected fluctuations in the timing, frequency and severity of events (including direct insurance and incoming reinsurance). • Reserving Risk: arises out of the volatility of reserves. • Accumulation/ Aggregation Risk: the risk arising from concentration of exposure in a particular geographical region, market sector or sovereign territory. See absolute risk.
Interest rate risk in the banking book (also referred to as IRRBB)	The risk to earnings, economic value and capital of the bank arising from adverse movements in interest rates. This risk is limited to the banking book and does not include the trading book (which is a market risk). The Banking Book relates to assets and liabilities resulting from non-trading activities.
Internal (risk and capital) Model	This is the firm's representation of the risk and capital management processes to support management of the business. The Internal Model is developed by the financial institution to determine the capital requirement on the basis of the company-specific risk profile. Defining and developing an Internal Model is a specific explicit requirement of the Solvency II Directive. It is, of course, essential for Basel II requirements as well as completed on a risk category basis.
Internal Control	An internal control is defined as the policies, procedures, practices and organizational structures designed to provide reasonable assurance that business objectives will be achieved and that undesired risk-related events will be prevented or detected and corrected.
Internal Ratings Based Approach (IRB)	A category of methodologies to the calculation of RWAs for credit risk (under Basel II, Pillar 1) and capital based upon the use of a bank's internal data. There are two types: foundation IRB (the firm itself determines its probability of default) and advanced IRB (the firm assembles all key elements of its credit

Term	Description
	risk model including probability of default, loss given default, exposure at default and maturity). .
Key (internal) controls	A key (internal) control is a control which, if all other controls failed, would detect and/or prevent a material misstatement. It may either be a single control that alone is capable of meeting the control objective and mitigating the risk or, in situations where no single control is capable of achieving the control objective, it is a number of controls that in combination achieve the control objective. An activity/procedure that if not present would significantly reduce the probability of preventing or detecting an error.
Key Risk Indicators	Key Risk Indicators (KRIs) allow the monitoring of changes in risk exposure and or breakdown of control, (for example, staff turnover MI may inform the assessment of the risk of loss of key staff). Ideally, these should be easily quantifiable measures (for example, failed trades) currently available to management. Key Risk Indicators should set thresholds to facilitate management response.
Lead Supervisor	The supervisor responsible for the supervision of a financial group or conglomerate.
Legal risk	The risk that the business is not conducting its affairs in a legal or compliant manner, which could lead to a breach either of contract or any other generic legal or regulatory requirement, such that the business suffers loss, or is forced to cease or amend its activities.
Likelihood	See Probability
Lines of Defence	A key basis of the Corporate Governance Framework. There are three lines of defence: • 1st Line: Responsible for risk management - Business risk takers have ownership of risk and primary responsibility for the management of risks • 2nd Line: Challenge and support for 1st line - Risk and Governance functions provide support to the first line of defence. This includes risk identification, assessment, evaluation, mitigation,

Term	Description
	monitoring, measurement and reporting.
	• 3rd Line: Independent supervision and assurance (Internal Audit provides independent assurance over the robustness of the risk management framework).
Liquidity Risk	The risk that a firm, though solvent, either does not have sufficient financial resources available to meet its obligations as they fall due, or can secure them only at excessive cost. There is also Foreign currency Liquidity Risk which arises where a firm faces actual or potential cash outflows in a particular currency which it may not be able to meet from likely available inflows in that currency or readily convert from another currency.
Loss events (significant events)	Identification of the cause of events (or almost, that is, near events) that will identify where business vulnerabilities exist and what triggers them. Details are retained in a loss database for decision-making and capital modelling purposes.
Loss Given Default (LGD)	The percentage of the Exposure at Default (EAD) that reflects the economic loss where default occurs.
Loss Scenarios	Loss scenarios are used to quantify the risk in the absence of sufficient internal loss data. The approach draws on the knowledge of experienced business staff and risk management to derive reasoned assessments of plausible losses which have low probability but high severity. Over time, such assessments need to be validated and re-assessed through comparisons to actual loss experience to ensure their reasonableness.
Mark to Market	Assigning a value to a position held in a financial instrument based on the current fair market price for the instrument or similar instruments.
Market Risk	The risk of losses arising from movements in market prices of financial instruments and commodities. It applies to both on-balance sheet and off-balance sheet activities.
Materiality	A threshold or benchmark level of significant and threshold matters that need to be brought to management attention. It is determined in both quantitative and qualitative factors.

Term	Description
Minimum Capital Requirement	The capital level representing the final threshold that could trigger ultimate supervisory measures in the event that it is breached.
Mitigating actions	The objective is to mitigate risks outside tolerance to the target level. The timescales and resources required to carry out the strategy should also be identified and agreed. There are a range of improvement actions which can be considered: Reduce, Transfer, Avoid, Accept. Key actions are monitored and progress reports included in risk reports.
Mitigating Factors	There are a number of ways to mitigate a risk, so it is important to understand what mitigation strategies wish to use. Those strategies may involve one of the four following options: • Transfer the risk to a third party best placed to mange it, for example, by taking out an insurance policy. Some risks, such as reputational risk, cannot be transferred. • Terminate or avoid the risk by adjusting the programme so that the risk no longer applies. For example, by removing those activities that would lead to a particular risk or stopping an activity due to its level of perceived or measurable riskiness/tolerance. Terminate the activity – not necessarily possible in the case of mandated or regulatory measures, but the option of closing down a project or programme where the benefits are in doubt must be a real one. • Tolerate or accept the risk which is basically the "do nothing" option, which means the programme will use existing management arrangements to handle the results of the risk happening. Typically used for "low impact" risks. Sometimes, this response can be just as risky as a more proactive response, particularly in an environment of constant change. • Treating the risk means controlling the risk by way of putting in place on-going actions, tasks or processes to monitor or manage a particular aspect of the risk. A risk is treated by identifying

Term	Description
	and implementing mitigating actions that address either the probability or impact of the risk and so contain it at an acceptable level. Controls tend to be the primary way of managing risks.
	Mitigation Actions, Internal Controls and Policies For risks assessed as being unacceptable (that is, breach of tolerance/appetite), clearly defined actions will need to be agreed to reduce the risk to an acceptable level. This includes identifying mitigating actions, internal controls and policies. Each required action must have a completion date and an owner.
	Mitigation can be achieved in a number of ways.
	• Avoid The business can avoid the legal risk by choosing not to take a particular course of action that would make such a legal risk likely to occur. This is only likely to be an option where no other course of mitigation is available.
	• Transfer The business can pass the legal risk (or an element of it) on to another party, via the obligations, warranties and indemnities contained within a contract
	• Control The business can implement a process that will prevent or detect the legal risk occurring. This may be achieved by requiring a regular updated analysis of the legal risk to be conducted, as well ensuring that the Legal (and Risk) function is regularly involved in all areas of business activity.
	• Accept The business can decide to accept a legal risk; indeed even after it has implemented other mitigation techniques such as control or transfer, there may still be residual legal risk that has to be accepted. Not all legal risks will or can be mitigated to a nil level so there will often be some degree of acceptance of a legal risk. It is important that the business understands the level of residual legal risk it is accepting after all reasonable controls have been implemented.
Mitigation	Limitation of any negative outcomes associated with a particular risk.
Near Miss	An event where there was a significant control

Term	Description
	breakdown but no significant crystallisation of residual risk cause an actual financial currency loss.
Obligor	The legal entity or person who has engaged to perform an obligation, typically to repay a loan or other financial obligation.
Operational Risk	The risk of loss arising from inadequate or failed internal processes, people and systems, or losses arising from external events.
Opportunity Risk	Type of risk arising from the (usually deliberate) pursuit of business opportunities, with the potential to enhance (though may inhibit) the achievement of business objectives.
Outsourcing Risk	Outsourcing risk refers to the risks associated with outsourcing key activities (for example, transaction processing or payroll) to a third party.
Own Funds (split between Basic Own Funds and Ancillary Own Funds)	Under the Solvency II Directive, Own Funds represent capital resources of an Insurer available to cover capital requirements (MCR and SCR). 'Basic Own Funds' equate to assets less liabilities in accordance with Valuation Articles, plus any subordinated debt in the business. Effectively on-balance sheet items Ancillary Own Funds' are any other item capable of absorbing losses in restricted circumstances and are subject to supervisory approval. Examples include unpaid share capital, letters of credit, and supplementary group support.
Own Risk and Solvency Assessment (ORSA)	Under the Solvency II Directive, the ORSA is the entirety of the processes and procedures employed to identify, assess, monitor, manage, and report the short and long term risks an Insurer faces or may face and to determine the own funds necessary to ensure that the undertaking's overall solvency needs (includes the assets necessary to cover the liabilities, including technical provisions, the regulatory capital requirements – SCR and MCR – as well as the internal capital needs) are met at all times. The ORSA can be defined as the entirety of the processes and procedures employed to identify, assess, monitor, manage, and report the short and

Term	Description
	long term risks a firm faces or may face and to determine the own funds necessary to ensure that overall solvency needs are met at all times. The ORSA is not subject to regulatory approval.
People, Process and Technology	People: The risk of loss (financial or reputational) related to the management and use of people, including organization structure, resource allocation, employee competency, staffing tools, management supervision, employee irregularities and compliance to HR policies.
	Process: The risk of loss (financial or reputational) arising from inadequate or ineffective design and operation of processes.
	Technology: The risk of loss (financial or reputational) due to deficiencies in data integrity, data security or technological infrastructure.
Pillars	The Basel II framework consists of three 'pillars'.
	Pillar One Sets out minimum capital requirements for credit, market and operational risk.
	Pillar Two contains requirements for the supervisory review of banks' capital requirements that begins with a self-assessment by banks of their risks and capital, contains risk management guidance for banks, as well as guidance to supervisors. Supervisors may decide that a firm should hold additional capital against risks not covered in Pillar 1.
	Pillar Three - which is sometimes called "market discipline"- Involves extensive disclosures by banks to encourage external scrutiny and comparisons leading to better risk management by banks. The aim of Pillar 3 disclosures is to harness market discipline by requiring firms to publish certain details of their risks, capital and risk management.
	The Solvency II framework has the same three pillar structure.
Portfolio Effect	The financial impact of the aggregated risk exposures will be less than the sum of the individual risk exposures. The aggregate risk is less than the sum of the individual parts, as the likelihood that all business groups, across all offices/regions will experience a

Term	Description
	worst-case loss in every loss category in the same year is extremely small. To adjust for the fact that all risks are not 100% correlated, need to incorporate a portfolio effect to ensure that the aggregated risk is representative of the total bank-wide risk. The process for determining correlations considers both internal and external historical correlations and takes into account the uncertainty surrounding correlation estimates.
Probability (or Likelihood)	The extent to which an event is likely to occur. In risk reporting probability it ranges from (in descending order in likelihood) the extremely remote to likely to happen.
Probability of Default	Sometimes called the expected default frequency The probability of default occurring for an obligor over a one-year period.
Probable Maximum Loss (PML)	Standard measurement in the insurance, real estate, and financial industries for quantifying risk due to extreme hazards and the resulting financial losses. PML is the anticipated value of the biggest monetary loss affecting a business and/or a building that could result from a catastrophe, whether natural or otherwise, called for this purpose a "maximum credible event".
Pro-cyclicality	Arises if the capital (or provisions) accumulated during economic upturns are not adequate to cover the risks materialising in downturns and banks are forced to recall loans to satisfy capital requirements. Banks' retained profits, which add to capital, are typically boosted in favourable economic conditions and rise less rapidly (or even fall) in recessions.
Proportionality	Means to adjust the size relative to other things. Therefore, all things being equal, a small FI with a simple business models and markets/products/ processes/ systems which are not complex would require a less substantial corporate governance framework compared with a complicated institution. An assessment as to proportionality is determined according to the nature, scale, complexity and impact of the candidate's activities, taking into account such factors as whether or not there is a limited product

Term	Description
	range, extent of market share and limits of geographical impact. The final decision will be based largely on professional judgement and assessment of the facts at hand.
	The principle of proportionality is invoked to ensure on the one hand, that smaller organisations are not overburdened, and, on the other, that multi-national groups can benefit from diversification.
Provisions	For Basel capital purposes, is the sum of all amounts set aside to provide for credit related losses including specific provisions, partial write-offs, portfolio-specific provisions (such as country risk provisions), or general provisions.
Prudential Risks	A company's prudential risks are those that can reduce the adequacy of its financial resources and as a result may adversely affect confidence in the financial system or prejudice stakeholders.
Pure Risk	See inherent risk.
Regulatory and legal risk	The risk of material loss, reputational damage or liability arising from failure to comply with the requirements of the regulators or related codes of best practice that oversee regulated business in whatever areas the organisation operators.
Regulatory Arbitrage	Is where a regulated institution takes advantage of the difference between its real (or economic) risk and the regulatory position. Regulatory arbitrage may be used to refer to situations when a company can choose a nominal place of business with a less onerous regulatory regime.
Regulatory Capital	The amount of capital an institution is required to hold by its regulator.
Reinsurance credit risk	Insurers assume credit risk through the use of reinsurance, with exposure to this risk driven by the amount of current and future claims payable by the reinsurers to their cedents.
Report to Supervisor (RTS)	Included in Solvency II's Pillar 3. The SFCR is for reporting all information necessary for the purpose of supervision including a qualitative report and using quantitative reporting templates.

Term	Description
Reportable Events	Events which must be reported under Risk Management policy or Company policy, legislation or regulation.
Reputational risk	The risk of financial loss or reputational damage arising from poor customer treatment, a failure to manage risk, or a breakdown in internal controls, or poor communication with firm's stakeholders or similar types of events.
Residual risk	The likely impact and probability of a risk after taking into account the controls in place, that have been designed to mitigate the risk to an acceptable level in line with the risk appetite of the business. In this case, you assess the probability and impact of a risk, taking into account the existence (that is, adequacy) and effectiveness of the controls and other mitigating actions identified. Thus, residual risk is the "value" of risk after taking account any mitigating controls (that is, inherent risk minus current controls). It is also known as the risk remaining after risk treatment. Many consider residual risk to be an expression of the current risk exposure of the business which indicates areas of threat and management focus.
Reverse Stress Test	The emphasis of a 'reverse-stress test' is on identifying the high impact stress events which would cause the firm to fail and considering the appropriate action, if any, to protect against such failure.
Risk	Potential of a deviation away from expectations, typically involving earnings or value in financial services.
	The uncertainty of an event occurring that could have an impact on the achievement of objectives. Risk is measured in terms of consequences and likelihood. Risk is all about the uncertainty of future events and how they impact the ability of the firm to achieve its objectives. Risk arises as much from the possibility that opportunities will not be realised as from the possibility that threats will happen.
Risk Acceptance	Decision to accept a risk.
Risk Analysis	Systematic use of information (which may include

Term	Description
	historical data; theoretical analysis; informed opinions; and stakeholder concerns) to estimate the probability and impact of identified risks. Provides a basis for risk evaluation, risk treatment and risk acceptance.
Risk and Capital Integration	Help develop best practices and consistency of standards across the firm • Provide challenge on the completeness, accuracy and consistency of risk assessments • Support to local management in identifying and evaluating risks, and advise on required improvements in risk management and control • Facilitate the development of a risk aware culture • Report risk exposures and escalate key risk issues as appropriate
Risk and Control Self-Assessment Process	(RCSA) An internal process for assessing current and emerging risks and the adequacy and effectiveness of controls.
Risk Appetite	Is the maximum amount of risk that a company is willing to accept in pursuit of its mission/objectives/plans. Sometimes, the risk appetite for the entire firm is called aggregate risk appetite. The aggregate (or total) risk appetite of the firm should be expressed explicitly and directly calibrated to the targeted financial performance indicators of the company. Or, said another way, Risk Appetite is the amount of capital that you are willing to lose in order to generate a potential profit – that is, the amount of risk a company, process, or activity is willing to take, while considering goals and objectives.
Risk Assessment (RA)	The identification and analysis of relevant risks to achievement of the objectives, forming a basis for determining how the risks should be managed. Because economic, industry, regulatory and operating conditions will continue to change, mechanisms are needed to identify and deal with the special risks associated with change.
RA, Evaluation	The overall process of risk analysis and risk evaluation, by which the probability and impact of

Term	Description
or Recognition	identified risks are estimated.
Risk Avoidance	Decision not to become involved in, or action to withdraw from, a risk situation.
Risk Convergence	Aims to align or integrate elements of existing risk, control and assurance frameworks to achieve more effective and efficient coverage as well as reduced complexity and management burden. Issues include: Duplication and overlap results in inefficient use of resources, Business fatigue due to risk management burden, Inconsistent and duplicative reporting to senior management, Excessive risk governance and remediation costs, Too much focus and attention paid to low priority issues and a Lack of comprehensive, transparent and consistent risk information. The benefits of Risk Convergence include: Benefits: Integrated process and common methodology for risk identification, assessment, monitoring, testing and reporting, common language for organization, risks and controls. Comprehensive and consistent risk reporting, Flexibility in addressing future regulatory requirements, Cost reduction through synergies and other efficiency gains and Risk management as a business enabler.
Risk Dividend	Benefits achieved by improved risk management practices, policies, procedures and tools. Benefits can accrue to one or more of the following categories of groups: Management, Customers and/or the public (shareholders or rating agencies).
Risk Drivers	Explanatory factors which help to determine the scale or direction of movement in a measure. These can be used to explain movements in tolerances, appetites and limits.
Risk Framework	The overarching environment that incorporates the risk and capital model and associated processes for the identification, assessment, measurement, managing, monitoring and reporting of risks.
Risk Identification or Risk	The first stage in the management of risks. As the aim should be to identify all significant risks, all relevant internal and external pointers (for example, processes,

Term	Description
Recognition	policies, business objectives, management information and reports, peer experience, stakeholder concerns) should be considered. Using a risk matrix will also help. However care should be taken not to recognise an unmanageable number, as this would result in risk overload.
Risk Limits	Is the translation of risk appetite into more granular constraints. The individual business activities' risk limits are established in a manner consistent with the overall risk appetite through a quantitative bottoms-up aggregation process.
	The risk profiles of the business units and of the overall firm take into account stress events in order to ensure that the firm is strong enough to sustain unexpected turns of event.
Risk Management	A systematic approach to protect the business resources and income against losses and unexpected events so that objectives of the company can be achieved without unnecessary interruptions.
	Risk management employs a set of tools and techniques which constitute a robust discipline, including the following stages:
	• Risk identification / recognition
	• Risk assessment / evaluation
	• Risk response
	• Risk monitoring
Risk Management Division	At the Head Office level, the risk management function has overall responsibility for risk and capital management across the bank, including Credit Risk, Markets Risk, Operational Risk, Capital Management and "Risk and Capital Integration (RACI)". In insurance companies this includes life insurance risk and general insurance risk. Reporting to senior committees, such as ALCO and Operational Risk Committee, the RMD provides the methodology and tools for identifying and measuring the complete risk profile, acting as a base for dynamic risk reporting and supporting management and lines of business risk teams in developing the risk management framework.

Term	Description
Risk Management Mandate	The mandate for Risk Management should describe its role, including independent, enterprise-wide supervision of the measurement, monitoring and reporting of risks and the determination of the related capital requirements. • The Risk Management Mandate needs to be aligned to the Risk Strategy with responsibility to independently advise, coordinate, control and challenge management and the Board, of the risks within the entity and as part of second line of defence. • The mandate should specify its authority and reporting lines, including escalating significant risk issues or concerns, whether raised by regulatory authorities or detected by RM itself. . • The mandate should describe the nature and timing of its risk reporting. • The mandate should identify the policies, procedures and standards and a measurement methodology that are congruent with regulatory expectations it is responsible for. • Other: Performing in-depth analyses of risks including post-mortem analyses of significant loss events, influencing/participating in policy setting by regulatory/external bodies and industry groups.
Risk Management policies	Policies that set out a series of behavioural principles and defined processes which apply across all applicable Business Units (BUs). • Policies that outline the risks under management and the key controls required to manage these risks. • Each policy should have has a functional owner who is responsible for maintaining and reviewing it and ensuring that the principles and processes are communicated and adhered to at an appropriate level of materiality. • BUs allocate policy owners at a local level to ensure that the policy requirements are fully implemented by the business.

Term	Description
Risk management System (Solvency II - CP 33)	The strategies, processes and reporting procedures necessary to identify, measure, monitor, manage and report on a continuous basis the risks, at an individual and at an aggregated level to which they are or could be exposed, and their interdependencies.
Risk margin	A generic term, representing a buffer above discounted best estimate cash flows. A risk margin may be used for various reasons, for example, to protect against worse than expected outcomes.
Risk of Ruin	Refers to those risks that can have a potential impact on the firm's financial position.
Risk Policy (Solvency II- CP 33)	Policies are internal guidelines established by senior management in line with the relevant strategies to outline the framework that staff has to take into account when exercising their responsibilities.
Risk Process	The key steps followed by individuals and departments in their day to day business designed to fulfil policy
Risk Profile	Common approach to the assessment and reporting of risks that could arise within business activities or external environment. The output of risk assessment / evaluation sets out the agreed list of priority risks. It can be presented in different ways including a risk register or bubble map.
Risk Register	A list of risks, identified by the business, that have been evaluated and require monitoring and management
Risk Response or Risk Treatment	The necessary response required to significant risks which have been identified and assessed. Responses should be proportional to the risks they address. Apart from the most extreme circumstances, it is usually enough to have controls that give a reasonable assurance of confining likely loss to acceptable limits for the organisation, programme, project, or operational environment. The risk response is the implementation of measures to modify risk, selected from the following: • Tolerate it

Term	Description
	• Transfer it • Terminate the activity • Take the opportunity • Treat the risk.
Risk Retention	Acceptance of the burden of loss, or benefit of gain, arising from a particular risk. Includes the acceptance of risks which have not been identified.
Risk Strategy	High level plans that are developed, that are developed by the administrative, management or supervisory body and are further specified via policies and business plans to ensure implementation in day to day business. The risk strategy should clearly articulate the 'risk' vision. The risk vision, in most cases, would be based upon the risk principles that are documented and operative. The risk strategy targets should have qualitative and 'soft' elements. And, the risk strategy targets should have quantitative and 'hard' targets. The risk strategy defines the company's attitude to risk-taking. Clear articulations of both risk strategy and risk appetite are key components in embedding risk management concepts across the organization. The defined risk strategy needs to contain descriptions of the risk policy objectives and instruments.
Risk Tolerance	See risk appetite. Can be substituted for risk appetite for specific risk categories, such as credit risk, market risk and operational risk. The firm's tolerance for risk and associated minimum controls are set out within the risk management policies. The variance a business will tolerate in relation to deviations from a target or maximum level of risk exposure, and could therefore be a limit (for example, no more than £100m of exposure to AA-rated fixed income securities) or a threshold (invest a minimum of £100m economic capital into insurance risk).

Term	Description
Risk Weighted Assets (RWAs)	Under Basel I these are assets multiplied by the applicable risk weights and the results added to arrive at total RWAs. Under Basel II, RWAs are calculated according to requirements. For credit risk, for the internal ratings based approach, includes mathematical formulae utilizing PDs, LGDs and EADs, and, in some cases, maturity adjustments.
Risks to Business Objectives	Refers to risks that could potentially impact the firm's future strategy, possible loss of reputation and ultimately future profitability.
Risks, Inherent and Residual	Risks are assessed at both the inherent and residual levels. The inherent risk is the risk before any controls or mitigating actions are put in place or the risk that the controls and mitigating actions in place all fail. The residual risk assessment takes into account the effectiveness of existing controls and other mitigating actions (for example, transfers of risk). Residual risk assessments are used for capital assessment purposes.
Sarbanes Oxley (SOX)	The Sarbanes-Oxley Act of 2002 (SOX), named after Senator Paul Sarbanes and Representative Michael Oxley, is legislation designed to restore confidence in the equity markets and in the integrity of financial reporting after several corporate scandals through a broad range of compliance measures that all lead towards greater transparency of information, accuracy, and accelerated reporting.
Severity or impact	The consequence or outcome of a risk. Usually measured in monetary terms.
Significant (loss) event	Loss event and/or near misses which provide a useful source of data on risks, for the risk profile, which have materialised and could recur.
Solvency II	Solvency II is a wholesale of the risk assessment and capital adequacy regime for the European insurance industry and establishes a revised set of EU-wide capital requirements. The Solvency II project was initiated by the European Commission in 2001 to review the European framework for the supervision of insurance companies. The key objective of the project is to establish a solvency system that matches the complete and accurate risks of an insurance company.

Term	Description
	Solvency II is based on the three-pillar structure.
Solvency and Financial Condition Report (SFCR)	Included in Solvency II's Pillar 3. The SFCR is for reporting required public disclosures including a qualitative report and using quantitative reporting templates. SFCR is an annual report.
Solvency Capital Requirement	The amount of capital to be held by an insurer to meet the Pillar 1 requirements under the Solvency II regime.
Standard formula (Solvency II)	Under the Solvency II regime, a set of calculations prescribed by the regulator for generating the Solvency Capital Requirement. The standard formula is the least refined method that can be used.
Standardised Approach	In the context of the Basel II regime, a risk-based model prescribed by the regulator for generating a capital requirement. The "Standardized Approach" is a simplified methodology for calculating Operational Risk Capital. In the Standardized Approach, the bank's activities are divided up into eight regulatory business lines. Within each business line, gross income is a broad indicator that serves as a proxy for the scale of business operations. The capital charge for each business line is calculated by multiplying the gross income by a factor assigned to the business line by the Regulators. For infrastructure groups a cost-based approach can be taken (or not).
Strategic Risk	Defined as 'the risk of direct or indirect loss resulting from adverse business decisions, improper implementation of decisions' or lack of responsiveness to industry changes, for example corporate strategy and industry changes'.
Succession planning and nominated deputies risk	The risk that, due to insufficient planning and/or an inadequate system of established "deputisation", a vacancy in a critical role cannot be filled satisfactorily, either temporarily or permanently, within an acceptable timeframe.
Tail Risk	High cost but low probability event.
Tail Value at Risk (TailVaR)	Expresses the expected (that is arithmetic average) size of the loss if it exceeds the Value-at-Risk threshold.

Term	Description
Take the opportunity	In addition to the other responses to inherent or pure risk, it may be possible to exploit a new opportunity resulting from mitigation or transfer, or to re-deploy resources freed up from termination.
Target Risk	The level of residual risk which will be achieved once all future mitigating actions are implemented.
Three Lines of Defence	see lines of defence
Tier 1 capital (under Basel II)	Represents Ordinary Share Capital, Distributable Capital Reserves and Profit and Loss Account balances as at year-end. Deductions from Tier 1 represent inter-group debtors (loans to other group companies) which are treated as fully illiquid for the purposes of available capital resources and counterparty risk adjustments.
Tier 2 capital under Basel II)	Represents all other capital not in Tier 1. While Tier 1 capital includes shareholders' funds (including retained earnings) and non-cumulative preference shares, Tier 2 capital includes cumulative preference shares, general provisions and subordinated bonds, which are classed as capital because they are paid after the ordinary creditors (such as bond holders or depositors) in the event of an insolvency.
Tier 3 capital under Basel II	Is comprised of items such as: unaudited interim profits and adjustments/provisions.
Tolerate the risk	Because you can live with it, or because the cost associated with dealing with it may be disproportionate – although you may still need to develop a contingency plan.
Trading Book	Consists of positions in financial instruments and commodities held with a trading intent or to hedge components of the trading book. To qualify, the positions must be frequently valued and the portfolio actively managed.
Transfer the risk	Transferring the risk means shifting the risk to the party best placed to manage it (in the case of financial risk this could be through securitization or insurance) but note that some business or reputational risks may be difficult to share or transfer in practice. Risk

Term	Description
	transfer can also create new risks. However, it should be noted that the transfer of certain risks is limited, prohibited or mandated by the requirements of laws, regulations or the firm's policies.
Treat the risk	Often the preferred option under various risk mitigation options - can be further sub-divided into four types of internal control. They are: • Preventive – these are measures taken before the undesirable outcome can happen, for example a separation of roles ensure actions are overseen and properly authorised. • Corrective – applied after the event, these may consist of contractual remedies to recover overpayments or obtain damages or may be a detailed contingency plan that will be triggered by the event (for example, disaster recovery or business continuity plans). • Directive – these focus on ensuring the right outcome, for example by insisting on the proper training or enforcing Health and Safety rules. • Detective – measures taken after the threat has materialised, for example to learn and apply lessons elsewhere, or a process of reconciliation of financial records or asset inventory
Unexpected Losses	Those that deviate from losses that could reasonably be anticipated (that is, expected losses) at a particular level of confidence. Capital is only required against unexpected losses in the credit portfolio since management builds expected losses into product pricing, provisions, and budgets.
Use Test	Financial institutions need to demonstrate that their risk and capital management internal model is widely used throughout the firm and plays an important role in their system of governance and, in particular, their risk management system, decision making processes and the Pillar 2 reporting (ICAAP for banks and ORSA for insurers)
Validation	Model Validation (for Risk and Capital Management) – Testing to ensure that the measures of the quantification of risks, such as rating systems, parameters or operational risk metrics, are accurately

Term	Description
	calibrated and are consistent with a bank's policies and procedures.
Value at risk	VaR is defined as a threshold value such that the losses on the portfolio over the given time horizon will not exceed this stated value at the given probability level.
Volatility of Risk	The term "volatility" refers to the actual and anticipated frequency and magnitude (or severity) of changes in the risk exposure under review. Volatility is affected by a number of macro-economic factors. The volatility of the risk under assessment will move up and down over time (sometimes more sharply than others). The frequency of the event details how often an event will occur (that is inherent risk), should occur (that is risk appetite), and is likely to occur (residual risk). And, the severity of the event is the cost that would be incurred if the event occurred (for example, measured as a percentage of the annual net profit after tax and dividend).

Lightning Source UK Ltd.
Milton Keynes UK
UKOW06f0158280214

227322UK00012B/37/P